RADICALIZING SPIRIT

Radicalizing Spirit

The Challenge of Contemporary Quakerism

Jeffrey Dudiak

Friends United Press

Friends United Press
101 Quaker Hill Drive
Richmond, IN 47374
friendspress@fum.org
fum.org

Library of Congress Cataloging-in-Publication Data

Dudiak, Jeffrey.
    Radicalizing spirit : the challenge of contemporary Quakerism
/ Jeffrey Dudiak.
        pages cm
    ISBN 978-0-944350-96-6 (alk. paper)
    1. Society of Friends--Doctrines. 2. Inner Light. I. Title.
    BX7732.D83 2015
    289.6--dc23
                                                    2015036344

Oh, my dearly beloved Friends, unto whom my Life reaches, read me in the covenant of Light, and Life, and peace, where our unity stands, in that which was before words were, and shall be when words are no more.

— Joan Brooksop, *An invitation of Love*, 1662

For Michael Dudiak, *in memoriam*

Table of Contents

Acknowledgements

Introduction
Differences and Divisions: Quakers and Christianity xiii
An Overview of the Project xx
The Future of Quakerism. xxiii

Lecture One: The Law Fulfilled
Is it Right to Heal on the Sabbath Day? 3
Remember the Sabbath Day and Keep it Holy. 7
I Came Not to Abolish the Law, But to Fulfill It 11

Lecture Two: Quakerism and the Fulfillment of Christianity
As Jesus to Judaism, so Quakerism to Christianity 23
Be Not Ashamed of the Gospel of Christ. 25
My Kingdom is Not of This World. 29
The Letter Killeth, but the Spirit Giveth Life. 32

Lecture Three: Radicalizing Spirit
Thy Kingdom Come 41
Those with Ears to Hear, Let Them Hear 44
Living Tradition as an Open Continuity 48
Radicalizing Spirit 50

Lecture Four: A House Divided
The Fractured Family of Friends. 59
The Unity of Mutual Commitment 63
A Living, Dialectical Tension 65
Risky Christianity: Losing and Saving 68
The Diversity of Friends. 70

Lecture Five: The Love of Knowledge

Radicalizing Knowledge 79
Behold, All Things Are Become New. 80
Whether There Be Knowledge, It Shall Vanish Away 84
Bear the Burden of Each Other's Failings, and Pray
    for One Another. 90

Acknowledgments

The following lectures (presented here edited slightly for the purposes of appearing in print) were delivered, one each weekday morning, at the 2012 Canadian Yearly Meeting of Friends at Camrose, Alberta, as the *Quaker Bible Study*. I am grateful to the 2012 CYM program committee for the occasion to address with them a long held concern that I bear for Friends, and even more grateful to Canadian Friends for the generous attentiveness with which they were received, and the gracious response with which they were met. The encouragement of their original audience was among my motivations to publish these lectures.

While these lectures were first delivered to a yearly meeting that would be predominantly situated on the "liberal" side of our Society, the lectures were designed, from the beginning, as an invitation to Friends from across the theological and political spectrum to enter into deeper understanding, and more vibrant conversation, with one another. So when the prospect of publication arose, my hope was to find an "Orthodox" or "Evangelical" Quaker publisher to demonstrate these pan-Quaker aspirations. I offer sincere thanks to Friends United Press for the courage to publish a book that I hope might respectfully stretch the imaginations of some in Friends United Meeting's core constituency, and draw in and challenge others as well. Indeed, this project is very much in keeping, I think, with the work of Friends *United* Meeting, in its ongoing (and profoundly challenging) attempts to bring Friends of highly diverse persuasions together for worship and service. Indeed, my role as Canadian Yearly Meeting's representative to Friends United Meeting (from 2011-2014), and my longing to make a contribution towards building up the foundations necessary to its important work, was among my motivations in the composition of these lectures. I express thanks to Annie Glen and Shari Pickett Veach, of Friends United Press, for their work in preparing this book for publication.

In making available a series of lectures in print form, certain editorial decisions need to be made. It is indeed possible to significantly rewrite the lectures in a form more conventional to a book, and in doing so one is able to fill in some of the "gaps" in the text; one is able to be both more precise, and more comprehensive, in what is being said. The risk of doing so is that the text can lose much of the freshness, and liveliness, that the lecture form affords (or at least should). Alternatively, one can preserve the vivacity and force of the lectures, perhaps at the expense of a tighter argument, by presenting in print the lectures in their more or less original form. Because this book is not intended principally for scholars, but for an intelligent and thinking broader Quaker readership who share my concern about the state of our broader Society, I have opted for the latter course, with all of the attendant implications, both positive and negative.

The epigraphs to the lectures, taken from the texts of early Friends, were added later, and are all quoted from Gerard Guiton's informative and helpful book, *The Early Quakers and the "Kingdom of God": Peace, Testimony and Revolution* (San Francisco: Inner Light Books, 2012), which I happened to be reading at the time I was considering publishing this book. The quotations are found in Guiton's book on the following pages: Brooksop, p. 270; Burrough, p. 201; Fox (1658), p. 278; Fox (1663), p. 121; Howgill, p. 155; Penington, p. 173. Thanks, Gerry, for the fine read, and for locating and highlighting for your readers (and now mine) these evocative quotations.

My thanks (as always!) to my family, Julie Robinson and our son, York Dudiak, who provide me not only with the time and space and encouragement to write, but also with a continual reminder of what's really important while I do. Additional thanks goes to Pendle Hill, the Quaker study and retreat centre in Wallingford, Pennsylvania, who invited me to present these lectures again during my stay there as the 2014-15 Henry J. Cadbury scholar. I was blessed by the rich interactions around this material that that occasion afforded. I am thankful too to The King's University, Edmonton, Canada, the institution at which I serve as Professor of Philosophy, for continuing to support and encourage me in my work among Friends.

The composition of these lectures was interrupted, and punctuated for me, by the death of my father, Michael Dudiak. The son of Ukrainian immigrants to Canada, my father grew up on a farm a few hundred yards from Pelham Friends Church in the Niagara Peninsula, in Ontario, Canada. Growing up poor, my father had a hand-me-down bicycle, one that was far too big for him. Thick wood blocks had to be fastened to the pedals so that his feet could reach them. With the help of a friend, my father could climb up onto his bike and get going, but if he fell off he could not get back up on it, and get going again, on his own. The Friends Church was on his route to school, and the (unpaid) pastor would often see my father, having fallen off his bike on the rough gravel road, pushing his bike as he went past the meeting house, unable to remount it by himself. It became his practice, upon observing this through the window of his study, to go out to the road and steady the bike while my dad climbed back onto it, and to give him a push in the right direction. They became great friends, and my father, as a child, became a Friend, a commitment that would sustain and animate him for seven decades, a conviction that shaped my father's life as much as anything, and perhaps more than anything. I miss my dad, his wisdom, and his indulgent love and support, and I am grateful for the continuing legacy and love of Friends with which he left me. This book I dedicate to his memory.

Introduction

Differences and divisions: Quakers and Christianity

I operate under a concern for Friends. We Quakers, despite a persistent emphasis on unity,[1] are a divided people. We are—to follow the standard designations—divided among Liberal/Universalists, Orthodox Christian believers, Evangelicals, and Conservative Friends,[2] these divisions being institutionalized (at least in North America[3]) into different Yearly Meetings that generally self-identify as being of one sort of Friend or another.

---

1   Unity has been a concern for Friends from the first generation of the burgeoning society, being one of the main themes of George Fox's epistles.

2   These four major "kinds" of Friends are distinguished, along with some basic statistical and geographical information about each, on the Friends World Committee for Consultation website. The standard language is to refer to these different groupings as "branches" of Friends, a metaphor that probably has its origins in, and has certainly been reinforced by, the famous illustration of the "Quaker tree," where the divergent groups are shown as having stemmed out from a common trunk. This illustration, given its ubiquity, and its effectiveness as a pedagogical tool, has no doubt exerted a profound influence on how we Friends think about ourselves and our history. The language we employ powerfully affects the reality that we live. This branches metaphor also, therefore influences, (for good or for ill) how we address the situation in which we find ourselves. The metaphor of branches growing out of a common trunk suggests to many that we will find our unity, if we are to find it, in "returning" to the common trunk that existed prior to the various splits—and so arguments abound among Quaker scholars (and to some degree also among Quakers on the benches) as to what the true nature of that shared trunk was (so that we can "return" to it, or be faithful to it), and this means that historians, and historical concerns, have to some large extent been at the centre of Quaker scholarship. This historical orientation is certainly valuable, even essential, but perhaps should not be the only, or even the principal, way to think about these issues. Without eschewing historical concerns, I seek another (and I hope complementary) route here, in keeping with my expertise: a more philosophical one.

3   In Britain there have not been any major and enduring formal splits among Quakers, in the sense that competing yearly meetings have been set up. It would be interesting to inquire after the effect that this has had upon the range of faith and practice among British Friends over against Friends in North America.

These "labels," like many such labels, are blunt in-
struments that often obscure what certainly is a far more
complicated and nuanced situation. Within each of these
standard groupings are Friends of diverse views and sensibilities, and so there is, practically speaking, considerable
breadth of orientation within them, and overlap between
them. Many Friends (myself included) are uncomfortable
identifying with any one of these "camps" *over against* the
others, and most of us (especially when considering ourselves) recognize that our lives are too complex to fit comfortably into *any* stereotype, however much we, as communal beings, require groups with which to identify, and
in the context of which our identities themselves continue
to take shape. However much they oversimplify, and however much we may eschew them, labels (that is, names and
categories that allow us to distinguish one thing from another) serve a positive purpose; we could identify nothing,
and thus neither speak nor think nor live, without them.
Though rough, these labels do name something real, give
us a way to identify what are significant and important differences among Friends, the acknowledging and naming
of which is central to any project of self-understanding.
There are differences—differences that matter—between
us, and we do well to acknowledge that.

But these labels, while useful, also name, reinforce,
and contribute to the perpetuation of tensions that historically have existed, and continue to exist, among Friends.
For better or worse, for better *and* worse, we have adopt-
ed these labels, and their implications. We live with them,
and by them. They help us to sort out and keep straight
what kind of Friends "we" are, but do so (too often!) by dis-
tancing (rather than merely distinguishing) us from those
other Friends, *over there*, who are not like us . . . and thus
perhaps not *real* Friends at all! And precisely in this way,

they divide us. That is, that part of the tradition that is particularly meaningful and thus dear to me and my group, and that our embracing of which helps to preserve and keep vibrant, gets taken by us as the core of the tradition, often to the exclusion or diminishment of countervailing emphases that have also been part of the tradition, and that are the more meaningful part of the tradition for others. So, while not all bad, these institutionalized differences among Friends are almost certainly not *all* good—especially when conflicts emerge, as they have historically and do to this day, over what it truly means to be "Quaker." When our differences are played out as mutual antagonism, we not only experience a tear in the Quaker body; that tear is, I aver, a blight on our testimony as well.

So while these labels—Orthodox, Evangelical, Liberal, Conservative—threaten to divide us one from another, they, nevertheless, serve the positive purpose of preserving emphases within the broader Quaker tradition that the adherence to other emphases, by other Friends at certain historical junctures, have threatened to overshadow, and perhaps leave behind. I am suggesting that the splits among Friends, that marked nineteenth century Quakerism in North America, and that established the landscape for Friends today, were not all bad; in allowing minority positions to be maintained against the weight of the majority (whether that be a numerical majority or a majority of power), a richer breadth of religious belief, spiritual practice, social engagement, and manner of worship, exists today among Friends, at least potentially, than might otherwise have been the case. The wealth of a tradition (its spiritual, social, and intellectual capital, in terms of breadth and depth of opinion, images, articulations, and concerns) is related, I would argue, to its ability to imaginatively *both* prophetically address *and* adapt to novel situations with their unforeseeable challenges, and thus to its ability to be faithful to its callings across shifting historical circumstances and cultural differences. Difference is good![4] One of the arguments of the lectures that follow is that we learn to appreciate and exploit that richness more effectively than we currently do.

But if it is important to respect, maintain, even treasure differences that matter, that are serious differences, how might we live out these profound differences in ways that do not necessarily lead to conflict? How do we benefit from our differences, rather than allowing them to divide, and conquer, us? Must we distinguish between tension and conflict, learning how to allow the former to unite and enrich us even while the latter divides and impoverishes us? Another thesis of these lectures is that a "living" tradition is constituted by a dynamic interplay between aspects that cannot be resolved into a whole that would still their interplay. The reduction of a tradition to a univocal and settled core truth that functions foundationally and creedally for all is not, I will maintain, the Promised Land at which those who would be faithful to a tradition should hope to arrive, but in fact the death knell for any tradition as a *living* tradition. In the lectures that follow I will argue that this is among the core teachings of not only Quakerism, but (as the pattern for the Quakers who followed him in this) for Jesus as well.[5] But this profound-

---

4   I resist the temptation to draw a serious analogy to our current concern with, and understanding of, biodiversity, except as a mere suggestion for further consideration.

5   A living, complex religious tradition is more like a braid (i.e., a complex of interwoven cords which mutually reinforce one another) than a single cord, which adds to both its strength and flexibility. Early Quakerism was not, on this view, an evangelism with social and political side-effects any more than it was a social movement that took on a mystical, religious form—rather, any number of diverse elements and concerns were woven into a complex whose vitality and energy was precisely the product of these diverse elements play-

ly difficult challenge of how to be productively together in and through the negotiation of differences is not at all unique to Friends; in many ways it is among the most important challenges of our age! One of the shifts from our "modernist" to our more recent "postmodern" sensibility is a shift from the idea that we create community by either *eliminating* or *marginalizing* difference to an emphasis on creating unity *across* differences. What a remarkable outworking of our peace testimony it would be to the wider world if Friends could model how to forge such a community across difference, even, and first, among ourselves.

The concern of these lectures, however, is not limited to the "macro," and rather abstract, concern about Quakerism as a whole (if there even is such a thing anymore!), but also affects, however indirectly, our own individual ways of relating to God, and thus our personal religious lives. We do well to recall that for all of Judaism, most of traditional Christianity,[6] and the broad swath of Quakerism, the principal actor in the drama that unfolds between God and humankind, and thus the locus of spirituality, is not the individual, but "the people of God," "the church," or "the blessed community." If it is true that none of us live our spiritual lives alone, but only ever in community, then the way in which we conceive of and live out our community has everything to do not only with the nature and quality of the spiritual life that we collectively live together, *but*

---

ing off of one another, gathered and deployed as a spiritual movement. It is that interplay (which I am referring to in these lectures as spirit) that makes of the movement a living force, a vital energy rather than a static entity. It is this to which I take the Biblical contrast between the living spirit and the dead letter to refer. And this, on my view, is why every attempt to identify the true (singular) core of Quakerism is a welcome and illuminating addition to our understanding, in highlighting the importance of some heretofore perhaps undervalued aspect, but ultimately reductionistic.

6 By traditional, I mean pre-modern Christianity, Christianity before it entered the phase of being (overly, I think) influenced by modern individualism.

also with the spiritual life that each of us individually lives. So while this is not a devotional book per se, it is an invitation to Friends to consider the broader contexts in terms of which our devotional lives are shaped and lived out, and that means, among other things, attention to how we perceive and function within both our narrower Quaker communities, and the broader Quaker community.

The more specific and immediate challenge of these lectures (which I take to be an example, and perhaps the central one, of the challenge of how to deal with difference within our Society) is an attempt to address the perplexing and often troubled relationship between Quakerism and Christianity in the contemporary Society of Friends, especially as that relationship is variously understood by Friends of highly diverse theological, sociological, and political sensibilities—often to the point of mutual alienation. There are, among us, Friends for whom Quakerism simply *is* an expression of Christianity,[7] for whom the idea of a non-Christian Quaker makes no more sense than the idea of a dog that is not canine. And there are Friends for whom the link between being a Quaker and being a Christian, where it exists, is understood as purely coincidental,[8] if not (for some at least) a remnant of Quakerism's most evolved and responsible universalist expression, and

7   Friends who hold to this view are less inclined than were early Friends to believe that it is the only true Christianity (Robert Barkley's comprehensive exposé of Friends' theological teachings, written a quarter of a century into the movement, claimed to provide, according to its very title: "the true Christian divinity"), but they have no doubt that it is a form of Christianity.

8   Many Liberal Friends maintain that early Quakers were Christians only because Quakerism arose in the context of a thoroughly Christianized society, and Christian language, the *lingua franca* of the age, was the only language available to Friends in which to articulate their experience. But, these Friends hold, liberated from that context, Quakerism is not bound to Christian forms, and the Quaker experience is able to find expression in other than Christian dialects.

thus one from which we do best to divest ourselves. As much as diversity can and should be celebrated, our divisions—and this one perhaps more than any other—have, practically speaking, made it almost impossible for us to work, and speak, and act *as a Society*. For all intents and purposes, despite some rare, fortuitous, if often haphazard, points of intersection, there is, properly speaking, no Religious Society of Friends, but a number of Societies of Friends (with some more comfortably religious than others, depending on what "religious" is taken to mean), often most militantly divided the one from the other around the question of the nature and status of Quakerism as essentially Christian, or not.

The lectures that follow are an attempt to provide a theoretical[9] framework in terms of which Friends from across the theological spectrum might find themselves in both more intentional and more vibrant community—or at least in a situation of greater mutual understanding and respect—with their co-religionists of other Quaker branches. It is also a personal account of my own struggles to come to terms with the contentious issue of the relationship between Quakerism and Christianity. Having been raised an Evangelical Friend, but having spent my adult life worshipping with Liberal Friends, and thinking of myself as genuinely belonging to, and with deep respect for the integrity of, both communities, I often find myself "between" Friends, caught up in the tensions that mark

---

9   My account here is not theological per se (the arguments about the possibility and viability of theological discourse being among the points of contention I here attempt to address), although I hope it is theologically sensitive. If it must be labelled, the account here might be closer to what was traditionally thought of as "philosophical theology," a kind of philosophical prolegomena to theology, a discourse that attempts—distinct from, but with an eye towards, theology—to understand the conditions of possibility for any meaningful theological discourse.

and often mar contemporary Quakerism.[10] This book is thus not only an expression of my work as a Quaker and a philosopher with a sense of calling to encourage meaningful interaction, and promote understanding, between Friends from across the branches; it is also a weaving of that concern across my personal testimony—and thus is intended not only as an invitation to thought, but as a solicitation to Friends to share their testimonies as well. My conviction is that we will be in a better position to submit ourselves as a Society to the leadings of the Spirit in whom we trust when our mutual antagonisms are superseded by a spirit of mutual listening, and mutual subjection—despite our differences—one to another.

An overview of the project

In the first lecture, in an attempt to lay out the dynamic that will set the agenda for the rest of the book, I examine the complex relationship that Jesus in the Gospels takes up with respect to the Jewish law, a relationship that he refers to as *fulfillment*—which is neither obedience nor

---

10   I have been thrown into the middle of these tensions again in the past few years in my capacity as the representative of the predominantly liberal Canadian Yearly Meeting to the predominantly orthodox Friends United Meeting (FUM). FUM is among a number of Quaker organizations that valiantly attempt, across deep and recurring frustrations, to unite Friends of highly diverse orientations in shared ministries. The challenges of doing so are substantial, and merely "holding things together" is often exhausting, requiring the expenditure of energies that might be otherwise invested, frequently to the frustration to those on all sides. I am among those who refuse to be convinced, despite much evidence to the contrary, that such an expenditure is a mere exercise in banging our collective heads against the meetinghouse wall. Might our diverse insights, perspectives, commitments, callings and gifts be understood as complementary and harnessed under the banner of a shared trajectory, rather than deployed in isolation from each other, or even against one another? I remain convinced that there is that which we can better accomplish together than we can in isolation, not as a substitute for, but in addition to all that we can and should accomplish separately.

disobedience, but, rather, and somewhat paradoxically, disobedience for the sake of obedience, or *an obedience that requires disobedience.*

My argument in these lectures is explicitly laid out in the second lecture, namely, that *the relationship of the early Quakers to the Christianity of their day can fruitfully be thought of in parallel to the relationship that Jesus took up with respect to the Judaism of his.* Given the early Quaker commitment to and immersion in the gospel story, we should perhaps not be surprised by this parallel. *Just as Jesus was a virulent critic of the Judaism of his day, but for the sake of Judaism!, early Quakers were virulent critics of the Christianity of their day, but for the sake of Christianity!* Just as faithfulness to God as embodied in Judaism required of Jesus a radical critique of a Judaism that had settled into structures that betrayed it, a critical-fidelity that (as we will have seen from the first lecture) Jesus referred to as "fulfillment," so early Friends sought to be faithful to the Jesus way across a radical critique of the Christianity of their day that had likewise settled into structures that, on the Quaker reading, had betrayed it. Otherwise put, *as Jesus sought to fulfill Judaism, early Friends sought to fulfill Christianity*—in a "revival" that simultaneously carved out a brand new future! Quakerism was, from the outset, a Christianity that was highly critical of Christianity, a self-critical Christianity, an attempt at the *realization of Christianity* that requires a *perpetual vigilance against any and every Christianity that would settle into an empty formalism* that threatens to sever it from its living Source: the Inward Christ, the Light that lightens everyone who comes into the world.

In the third lecture I examine this aspiration for fulfillment as a more general structure of human life in its very being alive, that is, as unfolding across time, and thus dynamically relating a past always open to the future to a future always grounded in the past. I re-label the term ful-fillment here as *radicalizing spirit*, describing it as *an open continuity*, and exploring what this might mean for the re-lationship between contemporary Quakers and our three-and-one-half century long tradition as Friends.

I turn my attention, in the fourth lecture, to describ-ing the relationship between Christ-centered and less- (and non-) Christ-centered Friends across my experience as a Quaker with deep and sympathetic connections to Friends groups on both sides of this divide, and suggest that we *re-think our aspiration to unity* not as an insistence upon agreement, but as *a mutual acknowledgment of the di-alectically complementary roles that Friends of diverse orienta-tions play in the living dynamic that is the radicalizing spirit of Quakerism*. If, as I argue in the second lecture, early Friends neither uncritically appropriated, nor disdainfully reject-ed Christianity, but sought to fulfill it, that is, to adopt and adapt Christianity across a creative transformation of it, might it be possible to understand different "branches" of Quakers as highlighting, as preserving through emphasiz-ing, different (but complementary) trajectories within the process of fulfillment—namely, Orthodox and Evangeli-cal Friends focusing more strongly on the "adoption" side, and Liberal Friends more strongly on the "adaptation" side? On this view *our differences are not an impediment to a vital Quakerism, but its very condition of possibility!* The life of the community is in this pulsating attempt, on the one hand, to articulate the meaning and implications of our in-dividual and collective encounters with the Christ within" and, on the other hand, the perpetual admission that all of our attempts to do so are inadequate to, and thus a restric-

---

11   This locution is itself such a limited attempt to articulate our Quaker expe-
      rience, and its adequacy to this task, and its meaning, is rightly in question
      among Friends (as it has been, for some time now, among Evangelical Friends).

tion upon, the living relationship such articulations seek (necessarily!) to express. Might this dynamic be expressed in the perpetual dance between worshipful silence and ministry, ministry and worshipful silence—where each becomes the context for the other? *On the Biblical/Quaker model, we can only be faithful to the way of Jesus by putting Christianity genuinely at risk*—requiring a deep act of faith, maybe even the deepest: faithfulness even onto the cross, across the *lived* reality of resurrection hope.

Finally, in the fifth lecture, I provide a reading of the apostle Paul's famous hymn to love from First Corinthians chapter thirteen as a way of *both* illustrating the radicalizing spirit of the Christian scriptures that founds (as this project argues) the Quaker participation in the same spirit, *and* as *a challenge to Friends to consider the difficult calling of loving one another—despite our differences and disagreements, and because of them!—as the very starting point for true unity,* as a means that is already itself the end at which it aims.

The future of Quakerism

Recognizing "the need to foster ministry leadership among young adults, and especially Friends," the Earlham School of Religion recently conducted a series of interviews and surveys among young adult Friends from which "two strong pieces of feedback" emerged: "a desire to learn more about the basic foundations of Quaker faith (that many felt had been absent from their education and formation), and a desire not to simply repeat old forms but take this foundation and build something that works for their generation."[12] Now in my fifties, I suppose I am

---

12 I quote here from a letter reporting on this survey sent by the Earlham School of Religion to the Friends Association for Higher Education executive committee, on which I serve. The survey was carried out in the autumn of 2012.

no longer a "young" Friend. Still, I resonate deeply with the concerns expressed by our young Friends—and consider responding to them both a personal obligation, and a wonderful opportunity. My sense is that these young Friends, across their responses to this survey, demonstrate considerable insight, providing us with an articulation not only of what they themselves desire (and we ignore the concerns of the next generation of Friends only at the risk of not having one!), but perhaps of what the Religious Society of Friends as a whole needs.

These young Friends rightly sense, I think, that the rich soil of tradition is not that in which we should bury ourselves, but that rooting ourselves in it *is* essential to the production of nourishing new fruits. I believe it incumbent upon us as the broader Society not only to respond with attentive generosity to that for which young Friends are asking, but to be with them in it, to allow their desire to give shape to our own projects. While the lectures printed in this book were written and delivered before the ESR survey was conducted, they might nevertheless be taken as a modest, but more or less straightforward, attempt to provide a response to the call issuing from these young Friends today. The lectures printed in this book are precisely an attempt to wrestle with the tension—which is here presented as a productive tension—between the spiritual depth of our past as this is embodied in our historical faith and practice, and the ongoing requirement to imaginatively address the fresh challenges of our future across sagacious innovations, and with how to translate the former into a resource and an inspiration for the latter.

Now religion in itself is this: the fulfilling of the Law and the prophets, loving God with all their hearts and the neighbour as self, and doing to all men as they would have men do to them, and not otherwise.

— Edward Burrough, *To the Rulers, and to Such as are in Authority*, 1659.

Lecture One:
The Law Fulfilled

Is it right to heal on the Sabbath day?

Among my favorite Biblical stories is the story of Jesus' encounter with the man with the withered hand. Most of you know it, I'm sure, but let me remind you by reading the story, and the run up to it, from Matthew's gospel, the twelfth chapter, verses one to fourteen (from the Phillips translation). Moreover, let's try and take the advice of the nineteenth century Danish philosopher Søren Kierkegaard and hear in the story, not a familiar tale whose outcome we know and through which we can therefore yawn, nor as an arcane tale from an antiquated book whose relevance is passé; but let us hear it as if we had been contemporary witnesses, as an ideological struggle, as a power play, as a matter of life and death, that is, as a moment of highest drama.

> It happened then that Jesus passed through the cornfields on the Sabbath day. His disciples were hungry and began picking the ears of wheat and eating them. But the Pharisees saw them do it.
>
> "There, you see," they remarked to Jesus, "Your disciples are doing what the Law forbids them to do on the Sabbath."
>
> "Haven't any of you read what David did when he and his companions were hungry?" replied Jesus, "—how he went into the house of God and ate the presentation loaves, which he and his followers were not allowed to eat since only the priests can do so?"

"Haven't any of you read in the Law that every Sabbath day priests in the Temple can break the Sabbath and yet remain blameless? I tell you that there is something more important than the Temple here. If you had grasped the meaning of the scripture, '*I desire mercy and not sacrifice*,' you would not have been so quick to condemn the innocent! For the Son of Man is master even of the Sabbath."

Leaving there he went into their synagogue, where there happened to be a man with a shriveled hand.

"Is it right to heal anyone on the Sabbath day?" they asked him—hoping to bring a charge against him.

"If any of you had a sheep which fell into a ditch on the Sabbath day, would he not take hold of it and pull it out?" replied Jesus. "How much more valuable is a man than a sheep? You see, it is right to do good on the Sabbath day."

Then Jesus said to the man, "Stretch out your hand!" He did stretch it out, and it was restored as sound as the other.

But the Pharisees went out and held a meeting against Jesus and discussed how they could get rid of him altogether.

This story is among my favorites because Jesus here is at his radical best, in the two senses of that term "radical" that I hope to highlight here in these lectures. For while he does attempt to justify himself, claiming for his precedents the superstars of Jewish history, and the stalwarts of Jewish religious life, Jesus here clearly *does* break the law, defiantly, and we know in retrospect the risks involved in doing so, as surely he himself, along with the others present, must have known at the time too. Jesus here is, knowingly, tugging on Superman's cape, spitting into the wind, pulling the mask on the old lone Ranger. Jesus is no idiot, and no innocent; he is a keen reader of his times, and knows full well that his message of gracious justice will provoke the ire, and the opposition, to the point of violence, of those who are benefitting from the existing system of ungracious justice. In the face of this intimidation, of this peril, Jesus doesn't flinch. Against the imposition of an oppressive order, against the stoning of the adulterer in the name of God, against the intricately structured temple economy, Jesus preaches setting the prisoner free, giving all that one has to the poor, and the remission of sins.

For those of us who want a radical gospel, an anarchistic and even revolutionary one, a courageous "over-against" opposition to the "powers that be" that defies convention come what may, here is our Jesus. I love this Jesus. This Jesus is one of the main reasons I continue to call myself a Christian, despite the fact that far too often, even perhaps most of the time, the dangerous name Christian has been commandeered by precisely the forces that Jesus here defies. That the irony of Pharisaical Christians is lost on Pharisaical Christians (that is, on most of us), that this oxymoronic reality is not recognized as such, has to be one of the great mysteries, and disappointments, of the Christian era. And we Quakers have not been immune to this seduction. We too love our rules, insist on their purity, allow them to decide who is in and who is out, and enforce them too often with self-righteous enthusiasm. But Jesus would have none of it. He likely wouldn't put up with much of *our* nonsense either. Most of us probably wouldn't like him much. Still, this Jesus is one of the reasons I continue to call myself a Christian, not because I share this courage, but because I wish I did.

But Jesus is more than brave, and defiant, here. He is also wise, and his response to the challenge here put to him, while no doubt brave and defiant, is also deeply nuanced. Jesus is no innocent, but neither is he a wrecking-ball; he is not out to destroy anything. For, entirely in breaking the law (and he *does* break it), Jesus also claims to be *keeping* it. As we have seen, in doing so he claims to be following in the footsteps of the paradigmatic figures of the Judaic tradition whose actions (based upon their status as honoured patriarchs) everyone would recognize as lawful. His attempts to justify himself are something like evoking case law over against statutes. That David, Israel's venerated erstwhile king broke the law too, and wasn't considered a law breaker, counts. So notice that Jesus is not simply introducing something new, something without precedent. He is not opposing Judaism, but calling it to its truest and best self, by calling his Jewish listeners to a radical re-visioning of Judaism based on a dynamic found within Judaism itself, indeed, at some of its richest, and founding, moments. It is this dynamic, traced from Judaism, through Christianity, across early Quakerism, and into our own day, that I am investigating in these lectures. But more on that anon.

So Jesus neither merely follows the law, nor does he merely defy it. He is neither a legalist, nor an anarchist. The Bible has a term for this nuanced relationship to the law that is *neither* obedience *nor* defiance, or is perhaps at once *both* obedience *and* defiance—where defiance is a certain kind of obedience, and where obedience requires a certain defiance. We find this term in its most straightforward usage in the Sermon on the Mount, where Jesus claims: "Think not that I have come to abolish the law and the prophets; I have come not to abolish them, but to fulfill them" (Matthew 5:17, RSV).[13] Allow me to call to your atten-

---

13   The passage continues: "For truly, I say to you, till heaven and earth pass away, not an iota, not a dot, will pass from the law until all is accomplished. Whoever then relaxes one of the least of these commandments and teaches men so, shall be called the least in the kingdom of heaven; but he who does them and

tion to this idea of *fulfilling* the law. Among the things that will occupy me in these lectures is contemplating what this term fulfilling might mean, and its potential importance to us as the body of contemporary Friends. My suggestion will be that Quakerism is at its best in replicating the pattern set by Jesus, when it is neither legalist, nor anarchist, but strives toward fulfillment. We'll get to that. But we must go back to the story to pick up some threads first.

Remember the Sabbath day and keep it holy

This story is complicated because it is not simply the case that the Pharisees are on the side of the establishment, and Jesus is the radical outsider. The Pharisees are themselves the radicals—well, one kind of radical. The mark of the Pharisees was their insistent opposition to any hypocrisy, which (as it does in any society) set them outside of the mainstream and opposed to the powers. Against the Sadducees, who controlled the temple and collaborated with the Romans, the Pharisees, and their learned leaders the Scribes, were the principled idealists of their age, who were offended at the half-hearted compromises and the pragmatic power of the Sadducees, of the establishment. They remind us of both fundamentalist extremists, and early Quakers!

There are, moreover, plenty of Pharisees among us Quakers today, on both the Orthodox and the liberal sides—those who are uncompromising in their principles and who work tirelessly, honourably and admirably to apply the principles in ever broader contexts and in ever

---

teaches them shall be called great in the kingdom of heaven. For I tell you, unless your righteousness exceeds that of the scribes and Pharisees, you will never enter the kingdom of heaven." (Matthew 5: 18-20, RSV)

more exacting ways, whether those principles be the apostle Paul's perceived advice to the churches regarding sexual purity, or an increasingly aware political correctness, or environmentalism, or—in some Quaker circles—an uncompromising insistence upon an increasingly detailed application of the peace testimony to ever more minute areas of life. What I am suggesting here is that the Pharisees, of Jesus's time and of our own, are not so easy to write off. In fact, we shouldn't write them off at all. The Pharisees are the enthusiasts, those who take up a cause and mean it, take it seriously, and work to see it through. They are good people, admirable people. They are the ones who mean what the rest of us say, and we need them. These are the folks we name to our committees!

Moreover, in reading this story we should be aware not only that the Pharisees were well-meaning and zealous of good works, but the Sabbath law that they defend was (and I am tempted to add "is") a law well worth protecting and enforcing. Far from being the arbitrary imposition of restrictions intended to cordon off a sacred time of the week reserved for an arrogant God jealous of worship and attention, the Sabbath law rather serves the most practical, and most important, of social ends. Against the avarice of the wealthy and powerful who might, if allowed, force the poor, who have little say in the matter, into relentless labour, seven days a week, 365 days a year, the Sabbath law is a stop. It is a way of building rest for the poor and powerless, against their oppressors, into the very social fabric, based on the model of God resting from creative labours on the seventh day.[14] The Sabbath law is a social structure designed to curb exploitation: the poor may not be worked

---

14   Although it is not entirely clear that the Genesis account preceded the law it is later taken to justify; it could well be that the Sabbath law inspired the structure of the Genesis accounts of creation.

to death; everybody gets some r & r for God's sake, for their own sake, thanks be to God. The Sabbath law brings life where there was death. And what better day, then, to worship God who both models and commands such rest. The Sabbath law illustrates the sacred in the best sense of something "set apart," a day set apart for the leisure of those who need it most, a day not able to be violated by the agendas of wealth and power. That's what it means, as the eighth of the Ten Commandments puts it, to "remember the Sabbath day and keep it holy." (Exodus 21:8, KJV)[15]

There tends to be a difference of interpretation around the origin, and thus the meaning, of such good laws. The more orthodox interpretation is that God reveals the law directly (rather in the manner that the law was delivered to Moses on Mount Sinai, literally, out of the blue), ready-made, and it is meaningful because it has been given by God, independently of us, and whose wisdom we discover after the fact across acts of blind obedience to it. The more liberal view is that we, across our own experience, discover what is good, and after the fact attribute this wisdom as having come from God, as a way of enforcing and backing up our discoveries with divine approval; we are so sure of the righteousness of this formulation that we label it as a leading from God, *as if* it came directly from God. In the first interpretation we relinquish responsibility for

---

15   The passage continues: "Six days shalt thou labour, and do all thy work: But the seventh day is the Sabbath of the Lord thy God: in it thou shalt not do any work, thou, nor thy son, nor thy daughter, thy manservant, nor thy maidservant, nor thy cattle, nor thy stranger that is within thy gates: For in six days the Lord made heaven and earth, the sea, and all that is in them is, and rested on the seventh day: wherefore the Lord blessed the Sabbath day, and hallowed it (Exodus 21: 9-11, KJV)." Here, then, is respite not only for the self, and the family, but for employees, and even for cattle, and aliens (perhaps resident or illegal). For everyone, and everything, as elsewhere we see that even the earth gets a Sabbath every seven years. Another version of this commandment appears in Deuteronomy 5:12-15.

the law, claiming that it is out of our hands, to be blindly obeyed, which is always at once both noble and dangerous; in the second we perhaps hubristically take the law into our own hands, make it solely our own, which not only makes it "relative" in the bad sense, but also places it too firmly upon the "worldly wisdom" that our Quaker forebears so distrusted (and perhaps justifiably). Part of what I am hoping to suggest in these lectures is that in a spiritual religion like Quakerism, we are best to reject this forced choice, this either/or. If we live with and in the Power of God, as the early Quakers might have put it, the distinction is meaningless. God need not intervene as if from the outside, because God is always already here, working in and through us. The outside is already inside, and the inside already outside. That there is "that of God in everyone" means that God is not elsewhere, but—insofar as we attend to this "seed"—already "with us," which is what the name Emmanuel means, and which is why early Quakers preached, fiercely and fearlessly, the Inward Christ.

But leaving aside the questions of its origin for the moment, let us reflect on the fact, necessary to reading the story well, I think, that the Sabbath law is a good law; it does precisely what the law at its best is supposed to do! The Sabbath law is precisely the kind of thing that Quakers both have and presently should desire, campaign for, enforce, respect, even love. Thank God for the Sabbath law, especially if you are poor. Our elimination in the last decades of what were once called "blue laws," in the face of consumerist and corporate pressures, means that many a single mother spends Sunday afternoons behind a jewelry counter, rather than in the park with her kids on a day when they are home from school. Of course, in our economy, this Sunday job might well be better than no job at all. Children need to spend Sunday afternoons in the park with their moms, but they also need to eat and be clothed. Nothing is simple. That's what Jesus sees here, too. Rather than accusing the single mother who works Sundays with violating Sabbath, as the Pharisees would have, Jesus would indict the system that forced her into this violation. Where the Pharisees enforced submission to the law, Jesus sought redemption, not from the law, but through it.

The irony here is that somehow the Pharisees, with all of their righteous enthusiasm (and I'm not being sarcastic here, their enthusiasm really was righteous), get things profoundly wrong.[16] What Jesus gets here (and we get too, insofar as we sympathize with his actions) is that the Sabbath is all about rest and recreation, rest and re-creation. The re-creation of the withered hand is precisely the point of Sabbath. Jesus has to violate the law in order to keep the law. This is the dynamic relationship to the law that is neither obedience, nor disobedience, but, I am suggesting, is named by the Biblical word fulfillment.

I came not to abolish the law, but to fulfill it

One way of thinking about this is as an appeal to a higher law. The Sabbath law, that is, might be taken as one particular instantiation of the higher law of, say, neighbour love, instituted at a social level. Jesus, it might be said, attends to this higher law, whereas the Pharisees are blinded to the higher law by getting hung up on one particular, and partial, expression of it, losing the higher in the low-

---

16 Both readers who love it, and those who reject it, need to remember that the Biblical word translated as "righteous" means "just." Some European languages retain this connection better than English, as *droit* in French and *Recht* in German mean both "right" and "law," where right has to do not only with being right as opposed to being wrong, but has to do with having "rights." Righteousness in the Bible has not to do with personal purity, but with justice.

er, missing the forest for the trees. But then why not just encourage and live neighbour love, and Sabbath will take care of itself? This latter gives us the anarchists' impulse, and there is something profoundly right about that. The fourth century church father Augustine (though far from an anarchist on very many axes) gives us the classical expression of this impulse with his distillation of Christian ethics: *dilige et quod vis fac,* "love, and do what you please." That's not bad advice; would that more of us would learn it, and live it. But we also know that love without justice is a mere wisp in the wind. Love is nothing if it is not concretized in the world, if it does not take shape in this structure or that. If someone says "I love you," but that love does not take concrete form in the world, it is, in other biblical language, but "as sounding brass or a tinkling cymbal."

Love is itself not a law, not itself a concrete form, but the motivation for the law, what calls us to construct good laws that protect, in the language of the Hebrew Scriptures, "the stranger, the widow, and the orphan."[17] "The law of love" is an oxymoron. True love is never an obligation, although there is no true love without obligations. It is because love motivates the law, takes shape in the law, but nevertheless is not the law, that the law can become empty, hollowed out, a mere form, loveless, an impediment to healing and wholeness rather than its vehicle. Justice brags of being blind, which is a good thing when it signifies impartiality, but disastrous when it means not seeing the faces of those upon whose weight it falls, for then we get Sabbath without re-creation, then we get not a day of rest but a day of wrath. Then we get no Sabbath at all, just the law, but the law without justice. The law is the body of

---

17   Concern and priority for those named by these terms, either together or separately, is a recurring Old Testament theme (that runs through the New Testament as well) but is perhaps first mentioned at Exodus 22: 21-24.

love, love's concrete presence in the world, but the body of law not animated by love is a dead weight, a corpse, which is why we need the police, but are so hesitant to call them.

The relationship between the law that love requires, and the way in which love must always transcend the law, is a complicated one. Love takes shape, "realizes" itself, in the world across structures like the law, but love remains irreducible to those structures, and goes beyond the law. Love judges the law, even as the law is the very reality of love in the world. The law without love is empty; love without the law is impotent. If Orthodox Friends major in "neighbour love" (as a correlate of the love of God, as per Matthew 22: 36-39) sometimes to the diminishment of a concern for justice, Liberal Friends accentuate justice (though sometimes coupled with a paradoxical anarchistic streak) often to the detriment of neighbour love. Of course the Orthodox want justice, and of course liberals are motivated by love, so those are blatant and rather unfair over-generalizations, but not without some basis in reality for that. If love and the law are interdependent, as I am arguing, then you can never have one without the other, but you *can* accentuate one of the terms to the point of eclipsing its correlate, to the point of perversion. One of the things I hope to propose in these lectures is that perhaps Quakers of very different orientations have something yet to learn from each other.

So, what does it mean to fulfill the law? It means to go beyond the law without destroying it or leaving it behind. Fulfilling means to go beyond while remaining within, both at once. Unlike in our colloquial usage whereby the fulfillment of an obligation means that I no longer have it,[18] the Biblical sense of fulfillment deepens our obliga-

---

18   Although there are such obligations, illustrated by early Friends who felt the need, for instance, to deliver a gospel message to some person or community, and having done so felt "released" from it.

tions, but in a manner that transforms them. In the Sermon on the Mount, following shortly upon his claim that he has come not to abolish but fulfill the law, Jesus ratchets up the law by engaging in a series of sayings that take the form of: "You have heard it said . . . (one thing), but I say unto you . . . (something else)." Thus: "You have heard it said to the men of old, 'You shall not kill . . ..' But I say to you that everyone who is angry with his brother shall be liable to judgment." "You have heard that it was said, 'You shall not commit adultery.' But I say to you that everyone who looks at a woman lustfully has already committed adultery with her in his heart." "You have heard that it was said, 'You shall love your neighbor and hate your enemy.' But I say to you love your enemies and pray for those who persecute you." (Matthew 5: 21-22, 27-28, 43-44) Fulfillment here means not that I am now no longer required to love my neighbour, or that I no longer need to be faithful to my spouse, or that I'm allowed to kill anybody. But neither does it simply mean that I am still to do the first, but something else in addition, too. In fulfillment, the relationship with the law is itself transformed. In Quaker terms we might say that the law is no longer something outer to be obeyed whether I like it or not, but that it becomes something inner. And this fits with the Old Testament ideal that the law is not some alienating code, but is to be inscribed on the heart (Jeremiah 31:33, echoed in the New Testament in Romans 2:14-15, Hebrews 10:16), or "internalized," in the language of modern psychology. The law fulfilled is a matter of the heart; if we don't have a heart for those whom the law serves we might obey, but we'll never fulfill, the law.

The point here is not to obey the law (although obeying the law is still required), but to be transformed by it, be made over in its image, which is what Quakers historically have referred to as sanctification or holiness. Indeed, early

Quakers, and many orthodox Quakers to this day, put a stress on "holiness," meaning being sinless.[19] Liberal Quakers often have an aversion to the word sin, as in our culture it has taken on a Victorian aura of personal moral impurity that offends our humanist sensibilities, but the Biblical term sin, *hamartia*, simply means "missing the mark," and Liberal Friends certainly believe that at least some people miss the mark on a rather regular basis—just listen to them talk politics for a few minutes. So perhaps, this early Quaker experience need not be foreign to liberals, either. In holiness, I no longer run up against the law; rather my actions conform to the law as flowing from a transformed self, one enlightened by Christ. Against the Puritans of the day whom the Quakers accused of "preaching up sin," that is, who taught that Christ's act of atonement was sufficient to *forgive* my sins even as I remained a wretched sinner, the Quakers maintained that Christ's act of atonement effectively *eliminated* my sin. If I couldn't be sinless, that is, if Christ's atonement left sin in place, that, they thought, was an anemic forgiveness. And many an early Friend went to prison for the blasphemy of claiming to have been transformed to the point of perfect obedience to the law, of being a very participant in the Life of Christ, of claiming to be, in their phrase, a Son of God.

To fulfill the law means to "fill" it up, but fill to overflowing, like the Biblical promise of an abundant life of cups running over (Psalm 23:5). The Greek word for fulfill, *pleroō*, has among its meanings in the New Testament not only to render full, to complete, and to render perfect, but also to pervade, and to abound.[20] Fulfillment is exces-

---

19   See Carol Dale Spencer, *Holiness: The Soul of Quakerism*, Eugene, Oregon: Wipf & Stock, 2007.

20   Joseph H. Thayer, *Thayer's Greek-English Lexicon of the New Testament*, Grand Rapids, Baker Book House, 1977, p. 517-18.

sive: violating all borders, exploding all boundaries, but flowing from the same source. The law *is* binding, but can for that very reason keep us in bondage. The law *frees us* (the Sabbath law emancipates the poor from the curse of endless labour), even as we are only free insofar as we are *freed from* the law (insofar as love so fills the law that the law itself cannot contain it). In a strange sort of way, fulfillment makes even the law obey the law. If the Sabbath law, designed for re-creation, prohibits re-creation, it is, even if kept, in violation of itself, and must, as fulfilled, be broken, in order to be kept, which is what the Pharisees, in their myopic focus on the law, couldn't see.

It is this dynamic of fulfillment, of forms that give positive and concrete shape to life and love, even as they cannot contain life and love, which I want to investigate in these lectures, exploring its implications for the ways in which we might understand ourselves as Quakers today.

Discussion Questions/Queries:
The Law Fulfilled

What are the attractions of legalism? What are the attractions of anarchism? What are the pitfalls of each? How does Jesus attempt to avoid these pitfalls? Might our culture be understood, at least in part, as a battle between legalists and anarchists? How might we negotiate the attractions of these conflicting trajectories, without being lured into either?

What did Jesus mean in claiming to fulfill the law? Is the argument of this lecture—that fulfilling means both obeying and disobeying at the same time—correct? How else could we, or should we, think about fulfillment? What might the fulfillment of our laws (both juridical and ecclesiastical) look like?

What are the strengths and weaknesses of the Pharisees? What can we learn, positively, from the Pharisees, and how might we avoid some of their shortcomings? In what ways are our churches or meetings "pharisaical," and how should we address these tendencies in ourselves?

What is "right" about the Sabbath law? What went "wrong" with it such that Jesus had to break it to keep it? How, in our day, might we institutionalize what the Sabbath law rightly sought to protect and promote, without becoming pharisaical about it? Is following the law (for example, the Sabbath law) good for us because it is God's law, or do we think of it as God's law because it is good for us? That is, do we obey the law because it is given by God, or do we construct our good laws in response to God's leadings? Is there a way of thinking about this that would not force us to choose between one and the other?

Is it the case, as claimed in these lectures, that "the law of love" is an oxymoron? What is the relationship between law and love? Can we have one without the other, or is love necessary to keep the law "true," and the law needed to give love concrete form? How do our laws (juridical and ecclesiastical) succeed or fail (or succeed *and* fail) to instantiate love?

Are we ever justified in breaking the law? To what might we appeal in doing so? Can we think of laws today that might need to be "broken" in order to be "kept"?

How does fulfillment transform our relationship to the law? Is the dynamic of transgressing the law in order to obey it only possible in light of this transformed relationship? What is required of us in such a transformation? How might the idea of fulfillment relate to the traditional Quaker emphasis on holiness?

What is the relationship between law and freedom? In what ways do laws promote our freedom, on the one hand, and limit our freedoms, on the other? Given this duality, what relationship should we have toward law? What is our responsibility in giving positive form to our laws, and healthy expression to God's law?

[The] Kingdom of heaven is seen, which is as a grain of mustard seed which is within, and many have received it, and are become as little children, and them that be converted into the Kingdom, they bring forth their things new and their things old; and many are digging in the field, which is the world, with is set in their hearts seeking for the pearl, and many have found it, . . . so the pearl is within you.

— George Fox, *The Pearle Found in England*, 1658.

Lecture Two:
Quakerism and the Fulfillment of Christianity

~

As Jesus to Judaism, so Quakerism to Christianity

In the first lecture I examined the relationship of Jesus to the law (and thus to Judaism). In this second lecture I want to examine the relationship between Quakerism and Christianity—and will suggest that as Jesus is to Judaism, so Quakerism is to Christianity. As Jesus criticizes Jewish formalism, so Quakerism is a criticism of Christian formalism. The antagonists have changed names: Quakers take on hireling ministers and religious "professors" (that is, those who professed the faith) rather than Scribes and Pharisees, but the structure of the two conflicts contains remarkable parallels.

I should admit at the outset that not only is the story I am telling here being staged (that is, presented in a way to highlight certain aspects for specific purposes, and allowing others to recede into background horizons), but that the stories upon which I am basing my story were to some large extent staged as well. I attended a lecture by a Jewish scholar friend of mine some years ago in which he opened up for the audience some Talmudic texts, and bedazzled us with the insight and wisdom of the rabbis whose discussions they record. At the end of the talk, he turned to his mostly Christian audience and said of these admirable rabbis: "by the way, most of you would call them Pharisees." In my first lecture I worked to show that the Pharisees were not the one-dimensional legalists they are sometimes pictured as in the Christian Scriptures, and that Jesus' relationship to them, and the law they championed, cannot be reduced to one of simple opposition. Though critical of them, he was as much with them as against them, or, as I have claimed, against them *in order to be with them.* The polemics (i.e., confrontation) of early Quakerism with respect to the Christianity of its day can be understood as similarly staged. Quaker scholars are for the greater part now convinced that what has come to be known as the Barbour/Nuttall thesis, that early Quakerism is best thought of as a radical form of Puritanism, has won the day over against the thesis of Rufus Jones, that early Quakerism was a species of mysticism.[21] That is, the Quaker arguments with the Christians of their day, like the arguments between Jesus and the Pharisees, were a family affair, and indeed, the viciousness of the broadsides issuing from both sides had all of the marks of a family feud. Quakers sought not to reject Christianity, but to call it to faithfulness, to fulfill it.

That is, I am drawing here a parallel: as Jesus sought to fulfill the law, which was with respect to the law neither an unquestioning and uncritical adherence nor a disdainful rejection or neglect, so Quakerism can fruitfully be thought (or so I am proposing) as a fulfillment of Christianity. As Jesus plunged deeply into the foundations of Judaism to call Judaism to be true to itself, so Friends sought to revive primitive Christianity[22] in an attempt to call the church to faithfulness, to call it back to the Light that had

---

21   The work of Rufus Jones remains impressive and helpful, nevertheless, and—especially in the broad way that he defines it—there is without question a mystical aspect to Quakerism. But that mysticism was the qualifying mark of Quakerism from the outset is doubtful. There were a few true mystics among early Friends, like Isaac Penington, but very few.

22   See William Penn, *Primitive Christianity Revived*, in various editions.

been eclipsed by the religious conventions of men.[23] And where Jesus saw that the fulfillment of the law necessitated the violation of any and all particular laws, however valid, insofar as they were lived outside of the spirit of the law, Friends recognized that faithfulness to Christianity required going beyond *any* particular formulation of it— even their own!

That is, I am trying to think here differently, beyond the polarized choices of either unqualified affirmation or outright surpassing, one of the most perplexing and contentious issues plaguing contemporary Quakerism—the relationship of Quakerism to Christianity. So what is the problem?

Be not ashamed of the gospel of Christ

When I was a boy growing up in the world of Evangelical Friends, I often had quoted to me, and was made to memorize, the Scripture (paraphrased,[24] from Romans 1:16): "Be not ashamed of the gospel of Christ." This charge was often supplemented, in a not so subtly coercive move, by a saying of Jesus: "Everyone therefore who acknowledges me before others, I also will acknowledge before my father in heaven; but whoever denies me before others, I also will deny before my father in heaven" (Matthew 10:32-33). The clear implication was that, on pain of my salvation, I was to boldly and fearlessly confess my Christianity, and thought experiments were conjured up to make this point: if a group of men came bursting into the meeting with guns, threatening to kill all Christians, would we

---

23 This non-inclusive language fits here; it was mostly men who promulgated these conventions.

24 That is, transformed from Paul's declarative "I am not ashamed" to the imperative "Be not ashamed."

have the courage to confess our Lord? Well, the men with guns never came. But that doesn't mean that my willingness to confess Christianity hasn't been put to the test. Indeed it has.

Frankly, over the years, it has become harder and harder to admit to being a Christian for very many of us, even for those of us who still long to do so. But that is not because we are ashamed of the gospel of Christ, but because we are ashamed of what all has been perpetrated in the name of that gospel. The Quaker historian Thomas Hamm quotes an unidentified Universalist Friend as saying: "The patriarchal Judeo-Christian tradition subjugated women, contributed to the imperialistic destruction of indigenous cultures, and fostered violence down to the present day." And given that it is "the source of pogroms, racism, sexism, slavery, colonialism, homophobia, oppression of the poor, and degradation of the environment," it is not surprising to ask with another: "How . . . can others claim to be Quaker and live a spiritual life devoted to such a Christ of constriction and oppression?"[25] Tom Hamm points out that this is an extreme statement even among Universalist Friends. Indeed, Christianity has also as often provided an impetus to positive social change, and hospice and grace to those most in need. But in our clearer moments how can we not admit that these Friends have a legitimate concern? How could anyone with any kind of commitment to the way of the gospel (the way of love, peace, justice, equality[26]) want to affirm any association with that? Christianity has indeed become so sullied, so polluted, by its implication in oppressive power structures, and the name so monopolized by those who wish to benefit by enforc-

---

25   Thomas Hamm, *The Quakers in America*, New York, Columbia University Press, 2003, p.125.

26   One could insert here whatever version of the Quaker testimonies one pleased.

ing them (whether sincerely or cynically), that it is hard *not* to be ashamed to be a Christian. Many of us quite understandably, and quite justifiably, run from that as from the plague it has so often become. In a recent conversation I had with a thoughtful and sensitive Friends pastor, he confessed to me that he thought that in America today it was perhaps impossible to be a pastor and a Christian, at least a true Christian; that is, impossible to be among those enforcing the power structures in which Christianity has participated and which it has perpetrated, if not initiated, and yet live the grace of the gospel. He was seeing exactly the same thing as the Friends quoted above who were antagonistic to Christianity, even if his reaction is to try and redeem, rather than jettison, Christianity.

If we are committed to gospel values (and it has been my consistent experience that all Friends of every variety are, although they are in each case refracted through different lenses, and therefore have different concrete manifestations), we have this fundamental choice to make: do we call ourselves Christians for Christ's sake, and attempt to reclaim the institution of Christianity over against those who would pervert it, or do we see Christianity as so corrupt that the only way of preserving these values is to reject Christianity, and the name of Christ too that is inextricably bound up with it, re-brand these values universal and human values, and happily let the whole Christian thing just go away? Is Christianity itself redeemable, or irredeemable? Evangelical and Orthodox Friends tend toward the first option, though many quite uncomfortably, and more Liberal Friends tend toward the second option, though most do not follow this road all the way to the end. I don't think there is any easy or straightforward answer to this question. I confess to going back and forth on it myself. It is important for me to call myself a Christian, but—

given what all has been wrought under the auspices of this name—I kind of hate myself every time I do.

This ambivalence about the institution, about the fixing of living faith in forms, is anything but the sole provenance of our generation, however. It is, in terms of Christian history, as old as its inspirational figure, Jesus, as I attempted to show in the first lecture, and prior even to that as old as the Hebrew prophets, who called into question the cultic formalities of the Israelites in the name of something deeper. Thus Hosea, speaking for God declares: "I want you to be merciful; I don't want your sacrifices. I want you to know God; that's more important than burnt offerings. " (Hosea 6:6 NLT) Isaiah is even harsher: "'I am sick of your sacrifices,' says the LORD. 'Don't bring me any more burnt offerings! I don't want the fat from your rams or other animals. I don't want to see the blood from your offerings of bulls and goats. Why do you keep parading through my courts with your worthless sacrifices? The incense you bring me is a stench in my nostrils! Your celebrations of the new moon and the Sabbath day, and your special days for fasting—even your most pious meetings—are all sinful and false.'" (Isaiah 1:11-13, NLT)

The early Christian writings set up a series of contrasts to name this distinction between the living and the dead. So we read, for instance, that "the letter killeth, but the spirit giveth life." (2 Corinthians 3:6, KJV) But even more deeply, and performatively, we are presented, in the image that anchors the whole of Christian faith, with the idea that "the Word became flesh and made his dwelling among us." (John 1:14, NIV) That's the way it is put in the gospel of John, once known as the Quaker gospel for the weight Quakers put upon it as the source of their own articulations. The same chapter significantly adds: "and the world did not recognize him," (John 1:10, NIV) setting up another contrast, this time between the Kingdom of God and the world. The idea here is that followers of Jesus are not to replace one set of dead forms with another set of dead forms, but are, rather, to be alive. The living Spirit of Christ, the Word, is irreducible to mere words, goes beyond the forms recognizable in the world, always exceeds the words in which it is articulated, and the forms that it takes. The living Word, the Christ, becomes flesh, finds concrete form in the world, but is not of this world; and his followers are therefore instructed, in a common phrase that is a remarkable distillation of Biblical teaching (though not found in the Bible itself), to likewise "be in the world, but not of the world."[27] In each case there seems to be the Life, on the one hand, and the form that that Life takes, on the other. The form that the Life takes is never to be mistaken for the Life itself.

My kingdom is not of this world

But that Life, within the Christian conception, does take definite form in the world, namely in the figure of Jesus the Christ—the very Word become flesh. The way of life preached and modelled by Jesus is not just anything at all; it has bite in the world; it calls Christians to live in this way rather than that. In a remarkable series of everyday and earthy illustrations that we know as parables, Jesus lays out a vision of this alternative way, which he refers to as the Kingdom of Heaven. "The kingdom of heaven is like a grain of mustard seed," or "like unto a merchant man seeking goodly pearls," or "like a treasure hidden in a field."

---

27 This phrase itself is not found in the Bible, and is probably based on John 17:15-16.

We contemporary folk often balk at the language of "kingdom," thinking it not only old-fashioned, but perpetuating an oppressive, hierarchical mindset we strive to leave behind, but it *was* a favorite term among early Quakers. This is in part because Quakers were not opposed to hierarchy, only to hierarchies among human beings. God *was* for them king; we were to be guided by God, not negotiate with God as with an equal. But it was also because they recognized that the kingdom of heaven spoken of by Jesus was not an *alternative* kingdom, but a *subversive* kingdom.

The term kingdom (*basileus* in Greek) in the Christian scriptures is a rhetorical device; it gives us the outline of a kingdom that isn't one. For those with ears to hear, as the Bible puts it, this is really quite humorous. A kingdom that isn't one; what kind of kingdom is that? This confused Jesus's followers at times, who didn't always get it, disappointed the Zealots who aspired to armed insurrection, and certainly confused the Roman authorities who saw it as a potential military threat, with the obvious results. Jesus's envisioned kingdom *was* subversive, but not in the sense of setting up a kingdom that would take on the kingdoms of the world head to head, battling it out with them for supremacy on their own terms, but in undermining the very idea of kingdoms as the world understood them. It was a kingdom whose weapons were peace, whose justice was forgiveness, and whose economy was grace. While Constantine in the fourth century, and a long, steady line of others since, sought to wed the kingdom of God to the kingdoms of this world (the ultimate power couple!), there has always been a smattering of God's people, sometimes referred to as a "faithful remnant," who have desired this *other* kingdom, and have often withdrawn from the world in an attempt to find it.

"My kingdom is not of this world" (John 18:36, NIV), Jesus says. But it is not "other worldly" in the sense of irrelevant for the world. Christians were, and are, called to live it out, to "realize" it, to make it a reality, to give the kingdom concrete form. For Christians Jesus preaches and lives that reality, is the form that the kingdom is to take in the world, but that is not the end of the story. Upon his departure from this world, Jesus promised to send the *Paraclete*, the Holy Spirit, as advocate or counselor (John 14:16, 26), to continue to guide his followers in realizing the kingdom that isn't one. Asking "what would Jesus do?" might be a good start, but it's not the end of the conversation. "What is the spirit of Christ leading *us* to do here, now, today, in this place, in the light of our present circumstances?" is a question at least as important.

Christianity inhabits the tension that is set up between Jesus's proclamation that "the kingdom is already among you" (Luke 17:21, NLT) and his teaching his disciples to pray: "Thy kingdom come, thy will be done, on earth as it is in heaven" (Matthew 6:10, KJV). Though grounded in and oriented by the form that the kingdom takes in the life of Christ, for Christians it is the living Spirit of Christ that animates and exceeds any form that Christian life takes. Christian life is only true to itself when it exceeds the forms that it takes in the world, even if to be realized it must take form in the world. The forms of Christian life are a response to the call of the gospel, the call to realize the kingdom, and so must take on some manifestation or other. But no manifestation is equivalent to the call to the kingdom itself, which always exceeds such responses, and refuses to allow them to settle into *final* formulations.

That's why even the apostle Paul, considered by many liberal theologians to be the enemy, the guy who ruined the beautiful Jesus thing by institutionalizing Christianity, is rather more complex. If out of the one side of his mouth Paul is full of prescriptions: telling women to stay silent in church (I Corinthians 14:33-35), advising deacons on their sexual practices (I Timothy 3:12), counselling slaves to obey their masters (Colossians 3:22); out of the other side of his mouth he is preaching freedom (e.g., Romans 8:21, Galatians 5;1), breaking down the power relations between male and female, Jew and Greek, slave and freeman (Galatians 3:28), and inviting the followers of Christ *to work out their own salvation* in fear and trembling (Philippians 2:12). That is not the blatant and obvious contradiction it seems to be, and is not so far off from what we find in early Quakers either.

The letter killeth, but the Spirit giveth life

Indeed, Quakerism was born of a disillusionment with the forms that Christianity had taken in the mid-seventeenth Century, and the experience of the Life they had obscured. "When all my hopes in them (that is, in priests, and preachers, esteemed and experienced people) and in all men were gone, so that I had nothing outwardly to help me, nor could I tell what to do," George Fox bemoans, before exalting, "Then, oh, then, I heard a voice which said: 'There is one, even Christ Jesus, that can speak to thy condition,' and when I heard it, my heart did leap for joy."[28] The language that Fox and other early Friends found to express this concern was that of a contrast between inner and outer. This metaphor was not meant to communicate topographical facts, was not meant to suggest that Christ was literally inside of them as opposed to outside of them,

---

28 George Fox, *The Journal of George Fox*, ed. R. Jones, Richmond, Indiana: Friends United Press, p. 82.

although the detractors of Quakerism often took it in that way, hearing in the Quaker affirmation of the Christ Within a denial of the historical Christ, and a few Quakers heard it that way too (though neither the majority, nor most of the principal Publishers of Truth). Preaching Christ as inside rather than outside could become a dead formality as easily as the reverse. Rather, this language was meant to capture the contrast between the living, breathing presence of God in their lives that caused them to quake, that convicted them and transformed them, from the inside out, as it were, and the fixed forms "out there" that lacked such Power. And this suspicion of forms continues to animate us Quakers today.

Yet while remaining suspicious of forms "outside of the Life," already in the first decade Quakers also recognized the need to give form to that Life in the world. They began to organize the people of God, which they did not hesitate to refer to as the Church, and to articulate (i.e., give form to) the Quaker experience. This did not sit well with all. Some immediately feared the return of the forms from which they had lived their Quaker experience as an emancipation. Some, like Perrot and his party, not only objected to the authority of the leading, itinerant Friends, but even objected to the setting of fixed times for meetings, arguing that Friends should trust the Spirit to lead them together at the time the Spirit would appoint, not any human conventions.[29] For good or ill, more practical heads prevailed. But the point is that the struggle between giving concrete expression to Quaker life, the pre-requisite for the life of the body as a community, the pre-requisite for *realizing* it, and the fear that those expressions would harden into

---

29   See William C. Braithwaite, *The Second Period of Quakerism*, Cambridge: Cambridge University Press, 1961, p.233.

the rigid structures against which Quakerism was itself a protest, was a deep concern among early Friends, and remains so for us.

One of the nicest examples of the attempt to negotiate these tricky waters is the letter to the Quaker communities "in the north" from the meeting of "elders and brethren" at Balby in Yorkshire in 1656, "the oldest church advice on Christian practice issued by any general body of Friends."[30] After laying out a number of directives, referred to as "necessary things" in the title of the letter, that ranged from the arrangement and discipline of meetings, to advice to ministers, to care for the poor, to domestic and vocational matters, to the relationship of Friends to the state, the letter famously ends with the following postscript: "Dearly beloved friends, these things we do not lay upon you as a rule or form to walk by, but that all with the measure of light which is pure and holy may be guided, and so in the light walking and abiding these may be fulfilled in the Spirit, —not from the letter, for the letter killeth, but the Spirit giveth life." These directives *are* to be followed, but not as rules or forms, but because they are *necessary* to the fulfilling of the Spirit in those who do. The Spirit requires forms, but is not stuck in them.

The form of our own more recent Quaker books of "Faith and Practice" echoes and extends this pattern.[31] In providing us with a series of evocative and inspirational quotations from significant periods and people in our tradition, rather than with a set of rules that Quakers must follow, we are presented not with a creed that dictates what

---

30 William C. Braithwaite, *The Beginnings of Quakerism.* I base my account and quotations in what follows on Braithwaite's account and quotations from the letter, from his pages 310-14.

31 Prior to the 20th Century, these books of "Faith and Practice" were referred to as the "Discipline" and were generally enforced as stringently as the name suggests.

Quakers *must* believe, but with an account of what Quakers *have* believed, not with a rule book for what Quakers *must* do, but with an understanding of what Quakers *have* done. But as we know, these "reports on past experience" are not insignificant to our ongoing Quaker life; our investment in them is not antiquarian, but futural. They invite us to find ourselves in this heritage as a way of moving forth, of moving into an unanticipated elsewhere. Like the letter from the elders at Balby of 350 years ago, they invite us to participate in the living Spirit of Quaker faith in a concrete, but non-definitive, way.

My suggestion is that we do well to understand early Quakerism—that is, the original impetus of the Quaker movement, that opens up the space and provides both the inspiration and the parameters for the subsequent unfolding of the Quaker tradition—as reiterating, at a radicalized level, as struggling with anew, the same dynamic tension between a living relationship with God and the necessary, but potentially stultifying, forms that we find in Jesus's encounter with the formalism of Jewish law. That is, my suggestion is that we do well to understand early Quakerism as an attempt to fulfill Christianity. But it could only be an attempt at the fulfillment of Christianity because Christianity *itself* struggled with the same tension, was itself such an attempt at fulfillment (though mostly a failed one on the Quaker reading), a struggle Christianity in its turn inherited from *its* progenitor Judaism.

It is, therefore, as much a perversion of Jesus to read him as either a wholesale adoption of Judaism or as a rejection of it, as it is a perversion of Quakerism to read it as either a wholesale adoption of Christianity, or as an outright rejection of it. My proposal is that we do not understand Jesus' relationship to the law unless we "get over" (in

the old Quaker sense[32]) the *false choice* between blind obedience and transgressive rejection, and begin to see this
relationship aright as the one that the Christian scriptures
refer to as "fulfillment," which is precisely transgression
for the sake of obedience, or an obedience that demands
transgression. Just as Jesus saw himself not as a rejection
of Judaism but as its fulfillment, I am suggesting that we
can only well understand Quakerism—a religious movement grounded in this Biblical dynamic to the point of
(unconsciously even) reiterating it—not as a rejection of
Christianity but as an attempt at its fulfillment—which in
each case means not settling comfortably into it, not "settling in" at all, but bringing it to life, by transforming it, by
transforming our relationship with it.

The possible implications of this reading for an understanding of the state of contemporary Quakerism I will
explore in the fourth lecture, but before moving on to that,
I will in the next lecture think again, under a different aspect, this dynamic of fulfillment as a "radicalizing spirit."

---

32   Early Quakers used the phrase "get over" in the sense of "get on top of," or
      "exercise power over."

Discussion Questions/Queries:
Quakerism and the Fulfillment of Christianity

Is it the case, as the author claims, that the relationship of fulfillment that Jesus took up with respect to the Jewish law parallels the relationship that early Quakers took up with respect to the Christianity of their time? What are the parallels, and what might be the differences? And, if this is the case, what should be our relationship to the contemporary form of Quakerism that we practice?

Is the adherence to, or rejection of, Christianity as "the truth" a good way of characterizing the disagreements among Orthodox and Evangelical Friends, on the one hand, and Liberal and Universalist Friends, on the other? How might the idea of "fulfillment" help us to bridge this gap?

Are there good reasons to be nervous about espousing and advocating Christianity today? Are there aspects of Christianity that are worth espousing and advocating? Is there a "pure" Christianity that can be isolated and preserved free of all of the worldly power structures with which it has become implicated, or is such "contamination" now an integral part of what Christianity *is*? Is Christianity redeemable or irredeemable? Beyond our personal and communal prejudices, why would we think one of these over the other? Is there room for "understanding" between people of good will who disagree on the answer to this question?

In what ways are the forms of worship in which we participate (our "most pious meetings," in the words of Isaiah) necessary to pleasing God (or participating in the divine Spirit), and in what ways are they an abomination? Is it possible to keep "the Life" alive in our forms of worship, or do these forms necessarily degenerate into dead letters? How do we give the Spirit form, give it a presence in our institutions, without killing it?

How should we understand the Biblical image of "The Kingdom of Heaven"? How have Christians typically understood it historically, and how is it generally understood presently? What is the relationship between this "gospel Kingdom" and "worldly kingdoms"? How might the employment of this term "Kingdom" stand in the way of realizing what Jesus was talking about, and how might it still be a useful metaphor for us today? Are we to understand "the Kingdom" as already here (as many early Quakers did), as yet to come, or as always here *and* always coming?

How does the Quaker distinction between "inner" and "outer" map onto the distinction between being in "the Life" and participating in dead forms? Is this a denial of the importance of "the outer" (history, the world, concrete forms of worship, etc.), or a way of understanding it differently? How should we think the relationship between the "inner" and the "outer"? How might the letter from the elders at Balby help us to better understand this issue?

Sing and rejoice, you children of the day and of the light; for the Lord is at work in this thick night of darkness that may be felt. And truth does flourish as the rose, and the lilies do grow among the thorns, and the plants atop of the hills, and upon them the lambs do skip and play. And never heed the tempests nor the storms, floods nor rains, for the seed Christ is over all, and does reign.

— George Fox, *Epistle 227*, 1663.

Lecture Three:
Radicalizing Spirit

Thy kingdom come

"The world is not as it should be." This is a judgment that we all share, Orthodox or Liberal, Conservative or Progressive, hopeful or despairing. And, constitutive of this judgment, internal to it, as its shadow, or its echo, is a prayer: "Thy kingdom come." That is, every time we make the judgment that the world is not as it should be, we have some sense, some vision, sometimes quite specific, but more often rather inchoate, of how the world should be, and we long for that, yearn for that, pray for that. Even if we have lost all faith in prayer, even if we cannot envision what the Kingdom might be, even if the "Thy" of "Thy kingdom come" has lost all resonance for us (even if we never had it in the first place), even if we despair that the kingdom (whatever it is) will ever come, or even if we cynically mock those who, like naive children, still believe in such nonsense—even if all of these conditions apply, every time we make the judgment, "The world is not as it should be," we say a prayer—voiced or not, believed or not, in the form of a prayer or some other: "Thy kingdom come." I cannot prove this assertion, but it is my wager.

And this because the judgment that the world is not as it should be is of a peculiar kind. It is not an intellectual judgment, for neither the theological teaching of Providence, nor Nietzsche's doctrine of the eternal return, nor Leibniz's philosophical proof that ours is the best of all possible worlds, can entirely still our minds about it, just as the scientific theory of natural selection cannot quite convince us that there is no "should" after all. Neither is it an emotional judgment, as our feelings fluctuate with our days and our diets, leaving us more or less hopeful, more or less optimistic, more or less energized, but not ultimately affecting our sense that, on a grander scale, things could, and should, be better.

Though I am struggling for words here, I am tempted to call the judgment, "The world is not as it should be" a *spiritual* judgment. The term "spirit" (*ruach* in Hebrew, *pneuma* in Greek) has as its core sense "wind" or "breath;" it has to do both with the principle of life, and with movement, with a living dynamism, which is why the Latin for spirit, "*anima,*"[33] is the root of our term "animation." I am calling this judgment, "The world is not as it should be," a spiritual judgment because as dynamic, or as the judgment of a dynamism, it does not, as do intellectual or emotional judgments, give itself to be stilled. Making such a judgment *moves* us, or is already a movement, towards something else, something that is not—namely, that which is traced out in the vision, the sense, the hope, however obscure, of how things should be, in terms of which we make the judgment that things are not as they should be. Our very judgment that the world is not as it should be draws us of itself out of our complacency with the present reality into a future that is not given to us even as it is our hope ("things *can* be different") and a promise ("things *will* be different"). Living our hope as a promise is at the heart of faith.

However dark the glass through which we see "that which is not, but should be," we strain to see it because

33   The masculine form *animus*, has overlapping meanings with the feminine anima (both mean "soul" or "spirit"), but the masculine form often has a meaning closer to "intellect" or "mind," the feminine closer to "breath, air, life force."

it beckons us, and we long for it. It won't let us rest. In the dark light of the judgment of a world gone wrong we see, as if in silhouette, a trace of what could and should be, and we know ourselves tasked with sowing the seeds of life that will transform what might be into what is. We all have a dream, even if our waking preoccupation with what *is* eclipses our facility to conjure it up.

Now there are, for those with eyes to see, at least as many reasons to lose hope in our hope, and to despair of the promise, as there are to believe in it. The idealistic ways in which we frame our various visions of the Kingdom might inspire us to keep trekking through the cumbersome muck of reality (and in itself that is worth a lot!). But these days we are mostly too worldly wise to believe that the Kingdom is actually coming, however good a show of belief we might put on in public. No biologist who has actually studied instincts (not to mention animal digestive systems) actually *believes* that the lion will ever lay down with the lamb, at least not past meal time. And at the end of the twentieth century, no historian worth her salt actually *believes* that nation states will ever beat their swords into plowshares. In the private councils of our own discernment of reality, we know that these are mere metaphors, ideals to *inspire* us, but not realities after which we might actually *aspire*. If the prospects of "hope and change" fill our lungs and imaginations with a revivifying fresh air for a season, four years later we know better. In the end everything reverts back to business as usual, everything reverts back to business, as usual. And if we are honest, even the most ideological supply-siders among us know that business is not the superhighway to the Kingdom either. As much as we want to believe otherwise, in our most sober moments we are more likely to begrudgingly acknowledge that we can't get there from here, and we lament with the Preacher of Ecclesiastes: "Vanity of vanities, all is vanity" (Ecclesiastes 1:2, KJV). And if at the turn of the previous century one could find a believer in comprehensive human progress on every gas-lit street corner, since the most recent turn of the century one searches almost in vain for anyone who still believes there is a correlation between scientific/technological progress on the one hand, and human moral progress on the other. We are left with little, if any, *reason* to believe that our prayer, "Thy Kingdom come," will be answered. The news is bad, and perhaps, getting worse.

Those with ears to hear, let them hear

But, according to the gospel, the Good News of the Kingdom[34] is not offered to those with eyes to see, but those with ears to hear (Mark 4:9, Matthew 11:15, Revelation 3:22). While we cannot *see* any way to get there, the Kingdom yet beckons us, *calls* to us. That's why the Scriptures define faith as "the substance of things hoped for, the evidence of things *not seen*" (Hebrews 1:11, KJV). That's why faith is not belief, and why if we reduce faith to belief, we strip it of what is most interesting and important about it. We only *believe* in things that are possible, things that we can realistically foresee; for *impossible* things, we have to have faith. And that's why the Danish thinker Søren Kierkegaard is right to assert that faith is both the hardest, and the highest, thing of all.[35] And it is the hardest and highest thing of

---

34 *Euangelion* in Greek (the prefix *eu* meaning good, and *angelion* meaning message [from which we get our word "angel" which thus means "messenger"]), from which we get our word evangelical. This wonderful word, that names in the New Testament the good news of salvation, has unfortunately been impoverished by a notion of salvation that is far too narrow, and unbiblical.

35 For a graphic account of this, see his stunning but troubling account of the *Akedah* (the commandment to Abraham to sacrifice Isaac on Mount Moriah) in his *Fear and Trembling*.

all because faith cannot exist in some nether realm where its pure ideality can be preserved against the ravages of harsh reality, like the pauper who closes his eyes at night and imagines his sack a princely robe; faith is only faith if it transforms this world, if the impossible becomes possible, if things in fact become as they should be. Otherwise is it not faith, but mere fancy.

The existentialist philosophers do a nice job of describing the dynamic movement at the heart of the human way of being, of showing us how we are caught up, in our very existence, in this tension between what is and what is not. Indeed, to exist is "to be" "outside of" oneself (In Latin, *est* [infinitive *esse*] means "to be," and *ex* means "out of"). Another way that this is put is to say that to be human is to have projects.[36] To have a project is to throw oneself forth (in Latin, *pro* means "forth" and *jacere* means "throw"), to throw oneself forth into a future that is not yet, but that nevertheless impinges on the present as integral to it. We are all here and now, in this place, today, but we are here to conduct the business of Canadian Yearly Meeting, and what we transact this week we transact for the sake of the future of Canadian Yearly Meeting as a whole, and for the sake of our testimony and ministry to the world going forth. That is our project; that's why we're here. The then and there is the very meaning of the here and now. What is not the case, what we are projecting, is at least as important to what is the case as what is in fact the case. What

---

36   Atheistic existentialists tend to understand that towards which we project ourselves as arising from our own desires, whereas theistic existentialists tend to see that toward which we project ourselves as that to which we are called, but the structure remains the same. Thus for Martin Heidegger, for example, "authentic" possibilities (or projections) are delineated by the circumstances in which I find myself, into which I have been "thrown" (*geworft*). Among these are the calls of God, an "already past" (God has always already called) from out of which I project a future. But there too, what is not the case is as important to human life as what is the case.

is not the case is as essential to human reality as what is the case, which is why facts do not have a corner on reality, and why science, while it speaks an essential word, does not have the only, or the last, word. Jean-Paul Sartre puts this graphically when he says: "human reality must be what it is not, and not be what it is."[37] The unreal future affects the reality of the present as much as (and perhaps more than) the reality of the present affects the future. We begin then to catch a glimpse of a circularity between the real and the not real, between the present and the future, that I am tying in this lecture to the notion of spirit.

But we only have this structure as human beings because we are temporal beings, beings who live in, and with an awareness of, time. Indeed, time itself takes shape across this relationship between what is and what is not. If we are to have time, we must have *both* a continuity between what was, what is, and what might yet be, *and* a decisive break between what was, what is, and what might yet be. If everything were frozen in perpetual sameness, there would be no time, for time is a measure of change. Yet, if every instant brought complete and total newness, total transformation, there would be nothing against which time as change could be measured. And that is why Kierkegaard (if I may refer to him once again) claims that eternity cannot be the same frozen as always the same, because that would be an eternity out of time. And, being out of time would be an odd definition of eternity, which should be full of time, always having more of it. Rather, eternity must be the perpetual possibility of a new beginning, which he refers to as "repetition."[38] Time itself, like the lives that we live within it, is an *open continuity*.

---

37   From Sartre's *Being and Nothingness*, quoted in Leslie Stevenson and David L. Haberman, *Ten Theories of Human Nature*, Oxford: Oxford University Press, 2004, p. 186.

38   See Kierkegaard's text of the same name.

At the social level, I suggest that "an open continuity" is not such a bad definition for a tradition. This is not surprising, because a tradition is an attempt by a group to move effectively through time. It is unfortunate that the term, tradition, has come to be associated with being stuck in the past, since the term itself suggests rather the opposite. *Traditio*, in Latin, from *trans*, which means "across," and *dare*, which means "give," does not mean to hang on to something, but to give it over, or pass it on. It names a gift that is passed down through the generations; it is not, as is too often thought, the tedious repetition of the same, but the perpetual re-generation of the gift. The giving of a gift has two aspects: first, it requires that I have something of worth to give, and, secondly, that I really give it, that I genuinely let it go. When I give a gift it now belongs to someone else, and they can do with it what they will, and what they must.

Conservatives and liberals are both bad at tradition in this sense. Conservatives hand on the gift, but at the same time refuse to really let go of it, and so don't really give it over at all. "Here is the gift, but you must do with it exactly what I did with it, and I am going to direct its use even from beyond the grave." This is in a sense what creeds do, at least at their worst, and why Quakers have always been nervous about them. This conservative gesture is well-intentioned, of course. We desire to give our children the best that we have; we want to save them the pain and the struggles that we went through in acquiring and formulating and refining the gift we now give. But this is a giving that keeps one hand on the gift, to direct its subsequent use, even as it's given with the other hand. It demonstrates a lack of trust, and a perhaps perverted sense of generosity; conservatives give gifts, but with strings attached. Liberals, on the other hand, tend not to give gifts, at least not of this kind. This is not because they lack generosity, but because as progressives they believe the new is always going to be better than the old, and why would we want to burden our children with our worn out, out of date, heavy and ponderous stuff when all the bright and shiny new stuff is waiting for them, just around the corner? Liberals are therefore also bad at receiving gifts: grandpa's creed is of no more value to me than grandma's couch—I'll get my own, thank you very much. But that also, sometimes makes them ungrateful for, or even blind to, what they do receive.

Living tradition as an open continuity

Okay, here's the rub. I have been trying, with all of the foregoing, to understand what it means to be part of a *living* tradition. I am proposing that we understand the larger Quaker movement as just such a living tradition, and seek to understand what it means for us, today, to be participants in it. One of the goals I set myself in preparing these lectures was the very likely impossible task of preparing lectures that could be presented at, and have resonance within, any of our Quaker yearly meetings, whether that be a yearly meeting affiliated with Friends General Conference, Friends United Meeting, Evangelical Friends International, or one of the Conservative yearly meetings, and I have, therefore, been attempting to speak (perhaps to the discomfort of some) in turn and simultaneously in multiple Quaker dialects. In this I expected to fail, and almost certainly have. But the goal remains: to try and understand the divisions within Quakerism not, as we so often do, as mutually hostile forces, or even as mutually tolerated solitudes, but as sub-movements within the larger Quaker movement. So while Quakerism is legitimately called a religious society, or participation in a certain set of practices, or adherence to a certain set of beliefs, or a way of life (depending on the predilections of individual Friends), it is, in the context I am here setting out, at least as legitimately thought of as a *movement*, that is, as a dynamic interplay between what is (and was), and what might yet be, between what it has been, and what it is always becoming. It is that tension, I have been suggesting here, that is *life*, and it is also the very life of Quakerism as a *living* tradition, that is, as an open continuity.

Quakers historically and in general have always been suspicious of tradition, because of its tendency to harden into the dead forms of traditionalism that quench the Life of the Spirit, even while Quakers of all kinds have recognized the necessity of this Life taking concrete formation in the world across a living tradition, even if across diverse groupings of Friends we have different ideas about what kinds of forms are most propitious for this purpose. But we all have our traditions, forms, that we think serve this Life; whether statements of traditional Quaker belief, like the Richmond Declaration, or the conservation of traditional Quaker forms for worship, like silent meetings. As suspicious as we are of traditionalism, we all preserve and perpetuate something of the tradition, or else we wouldn't recognize ourselves as Friends. Indeed, while we hope to be open to new light as we deliberate over important issues at this yearly meeting, we also know that we are not open to just anything; certain ideas might well be deemed to be not in the Spirit of Friends, and even certain procedures deemed to be out of "gospel order."

A tradition remains a living tradition, then, only if there is an open continuity, only if the forms in which we live are of themselves open to renewal, and only if the innovative is consistent with what has opened on to it, without being determined by it—for then it would not be truly innovative, but just more of the same. The idea of an open continuity that I have explored in this lecture is, I am proposing, parallel to the biblical idea of "fulfillment" that I looked at in the opening two lectures. In each case we have a structure, or a form, that is established as a response to some call to Life, which has to be perpetually re-visioned if it is to remain a responsible response to that call, and not sink into a self-satisfied immobility. I would now like to re-brand this notion of an open continuity, this dynamic of fulfillment, with a term I hope will resonate with Quakers, and will open yet another vista upon the larger framework I am suggesting as a way of understanding our respective places within the larger Quaker movement. The term I would like to suggest is "radicalizing spirit."

Radicalizing Spirit

Indeed, the term "radical" harbors a wonderful ambiguity. The etymological origin of the term radical is the Latin *radix*, which means root. Among the dictionary meanings of radical is the following: "forming an inherent or fundamental part of the nature of someone or something." Here, then, something is at its most radical when it is rooted most securely in what it is. But the term also has taken on another meaning, obviously related to, but seemingly contradictory to the first. On this meaning, radical refers to a change or action "relating to or affecting the fundamental nature of something," and it is this meaning that gives us radical in the sense of something "characterized by departure from tradition; innovative or progressive," and as "advocating a thorough or complete political or social reform." The term radical can mean *either* being deeply rooted, *or* tearing something up from the roots. It can mean *either* being bound firmly and securely to its ground, *or* being liberated from such an attachment altogether.

What I am working toward suggesting in these lectures is that this either/or is perhaps a false choice, and that we might do well to think in terms of both/and, that is, that these two senses of radical are not disjunctive, are not actually opposed to one another, but depend upon each other. In philosophy we refer to this kind of mutually dependent relationship between terms in tension as a dialectical one (in Greek, *dia* means "through," and *legein* means "to speak"), which means that the two senses of the term are in conversation with one another, answer to one another. So just as for Jesus, fidelity to the law meant that the law needed to be opened up, driven beyond itself, so for early Quakers, fidelity to the Spirit of Christ meant that Christianity needed to be opened up, driven beyond itself.

What I am suggesting in this lecture is that this structure is not unique to Jesus, or to Quakers, but is part and parcel of what it means to be alive. Life is alive, is animated, by the dialectical relationship between "what is" and "what is not, but should be," between the past and the future, between, on the one hand, the grounding practices and, on the other hand, the aspirations of a living tradition.

In this context I would like to suggest that we can understand the term "spirit" to name this restless circulation between "what is" and "what might be, what should be, what must be." The spirit of something names the way in which this dynamic, this interplay of open continuity, is taken up in any particular case. A spiritual movement is one in which the structures of a particular movement open up upon new possibilities that in being realized transform the original structures themselves, which in turn open up upon yet again further new possibilities. Our understandings of ourselves open up new possibilities for re-forming our world, which in turn transform our understandings of ourselves, which in turn open up yet other new possibilities to be realized. That is what it means to be "alive" in a *spiritual* sense.[39] And this is why we speak of spiritual *movements*. Spirits are on the move, are restless, like everyone born of the Spirit who, according to John's gospel, is like the wind that "bloweth where it listeth" (John 3:8, KJV), in defiance of *all* of our expectations. That's why trusting spirits is always a matter of faith. Not quite formless, but living beyond their forms, restlessly seeking forms from which they are perpetually expelled, spirits seem simultaneously to be and not to be, inhabit the inter-spaces between being and not being, which is why we associate spirits with ghosts and spectres. I do not believe in ghosts, but I do believe we are called to discern spirits—a practice long at the heart of Quakerism. For not all spirits are holy spirits. The restless circulation between "what is" and "what yet might be" creates an energy, energies in which we, as spiritual beings, get caught up: the spirit of the Olympics; the spirit of capitalism; the spirit of Quakerism. The spirits in which we participate, the new possibilities that we realize in continuity with who are already are, constitute the textures of our lives. If the realization of possibilities into actualities opens up new possibilities that in turn allow for richer actualities, *per infinitum*, we have a living, or a holy spirit, the spirit of Life, but where the realization of possibilities

---

39 The New Testament Greek has two words for life, *bios*, which refers to the life of an organism, and is the foundation of the term biology, which studies such organisms, and *zoē*, which refers to the spiritual life of a person (or of God). I do not think this is based on a dualism, as if the body and spirit were separate entities each with their own kind of being alive, but rather suggests that there are different ways that we as animated bodies find life. We all know the experience of being quite healthy of body but discouraged in spirit, or being physically unwell but still feeling strangely "full of life."

closes down the potential for further possibilities, which in turn impoverishes our actuality, we are faced with the spirit of death.

If we are to understand Quakerism as a living tradition, I suggest we understand it across its radicalizing spirit, that is, across the dialectical tension between the forms it has taken, its "radicality" in the sense of being "rooted," and the ever new potentialities opened up by these forms, without being contained within them, its "radicality" in the sense of ongoing and fundamental transformation. A living tradition can no more leave the forms in which it is realized behind than it can settle comfortably into them. They in their turn are transformed by the possibilities opened up across them. They are fulfilled, which means that they are neither abandoned nor do they stay the same. That, at least, was the suggestion of the previous lecture. Indeed, the important and perplexing issue of the relationship of Quakerism to Christianity, which I will take up again in the next lecture, I am trying to illuminate against the background of this idea of Quakerism as a radicalizing spirit.

By way of anticipation, I would like here to borrow a formula from a recent book that grew out of a seminar held at the Woodbrooke Quaker Study Centre in Birmingham, England, staged to encourage an open and honest discussion around the identity of Quakerism between a Christian Quaker, Timothy Ashworth, and Alex Wildwood, representing emerging, other-than-Christian, expressions of Quaker faith. The title of their book, and the formula I would like to borrow, is: *Rooted in Christianity, Open to New Light*.[40] I think this description of Quakerism apt, and true,

---

40   Timothy Ashworth and Alex Wildwood, *Rooted in Christianity, Open to New Light: Quaker Spiritual Diverstiy*, London: Pronoun Press in partnership with Woodbrooke Quaker Study Centre, 2009. Although the phrase "open to new

both in an historical/sociological sense, and in a spiritual sense. Part of what I am aiming at in these lectures is to propose a theoretical framework that will allow us to understand the two sides of this description not disjunctively, but as forming a coherence, not as divided, but as distinct but interrelated "moments" within a larger whole.

---

light" as a description of Quakerism and as a prevailing emphasis within it (especially if it is taken to override a simultaneous rootedness) is a twentieth century innovation, I believe it does identify a trajectory that has been a part of the Quaker movement from the beginning, as I suggest throughout these lectures.

Discussion Questions/Queries:
Radicalizing Spirit

What is prayer? Is prayer, as described in this lecture (that is, as an expression of our longing that things be as they should be rather than as they are), a specific activity among others, or a basic and universal aspect of human life, such that we all live our lives as a prayer, whether we acknowledge it or not? If the latter, how might this affect how we engage in the *activity* of prayer? Might this allow those who "don't believe in prayer" to see what, merely as living, they are already "praying" for? And might this allow those who do pray to more fully respond to the Biblical mandate to "pray without ceasing"?

Do we need to distinguish between faith and belief? If they are to be distinguished, how would each be characterized? What does each have that the other lacks? Which of the two is more important to religious life, and why? How might this distinction help us to more fully and faithfully encounter those who do not share our beliefs?

How important are "traditions" to our lives, and especially to our lives as Friends? Do we need them? What positive purpose do they serve? What do they sometimes get in the way of? Is an "open continuity" a faithful way to describe a tradition as a "living tradition"? What do conservatives understand about traditions that liberals tend to miss, and what do liberals understand about traditions that conservatives tend to miss? What distinguishes tradition from traditionalism? How do we keep our traditions alive?

If we were to think of Quakerism as a "movement" (that is, as a "living tradition"), how would that change the way that we think of ourselves within it, and the way we live it out? Would a definitive interpretation of that tradition become less important? Would the necessity of perpetually (re)interpreting the tradition—especially in light of ever changing cultural situations—become more important? Would this make it easier to see other Friends, who do not share our interpretation of Quakerism, as nevertheless participants in the same movement?

Is the term "spirit" a good way of naming the "restless circulation" between what is and what should be? How might recognizing ourselves as fundamentally "spiritual" beings (in this sense), who by nature get caught up in spiritual movements, affect the way in which we live our lives? How are we to discern evil spirits from holy spirits, oppressive from life-enhancing spirits? What might the Biblical reference to the Holy Spirit have to do with this?

And from that day forward our hearts were knit unto the Lord, and one unto another in true and fervent love, not by any external covenant or external form but we entered into the covenant of Life with God. And that was as a strong obligation or bond upon all our spirits which united us one unto another ... in the unity of the Spirit and of the bond of peace.

— Francis Howgill, *A Testimony Concerning ...*
Edward Burroughs, 1662.

Lecture Four:
Quakerism: A House Divided

The fractured family of Friends

This is the fourth of my five lectures, and it's time I came clean. This reading of Quakerism as an attempt at fulfilling Christianity, or again, as a radicalizing spirit, is a motivated reading, one designed to serve a particular purpose. I don't feel badly about that, as I think that all readings are motivated readings. But I do want to be honest about my motivation. My motivation is to promote respectful and open dialogue, *and* mutual learning—especially at a spiritual level—between what have long been, and sadly too often still remain, largely antagonistic branches of Quakers. There is much at stake for very many of us in such conversations, and so some of what I want to say is hard to say, *and* hard to hear. I say it humbly, and with some fear and trembling. It is profoundly important for me, therefore, to say what I have to say in the right spirit, a spirit of generosity and love, and I pray Friends hear it in the spirit in which it is offered—not as an accusation, but as an invitation to Friends to engage in the always difficult, but also glorious, task of examining our own prejudices.

Part of this motivation, of seeking healthier relationships between diverse groupings of Friends, is autobiographical, so what I have to say is coloured by my own experience. I am a lifelong Friend, with deep ties and commitment to Quakerism, and its potential for contributing to what early Friends would not have hesitated to call the Kingdom of God,[41] a potential marred, on my view at least, by the way in which we live our divisions. I personally have lived these divisions, and live in them still. I was raised an Evangelical Friend, in a small Quaker meeting in southern Ontario that was one of the few that refused membership in Canadian Yearly Meeting when, in 1955, the then Hicksite, Orthodox, and Wilberite yearly meetings in Canada re-united into our current CYM. My father was a young man at the time, and while largely led by others of riper age and experience, was among the team who, fearing for the Christian character of the local meeting, declined to join CYM. When I first encountered CYM folks some quarter of a century ago, there were some old timers who still remembered my father—as difficult, as the opposition. So I was raised a Friend, but one with suspicions about Liberal Friends, and my attendance at an Evangelical Friends university did little to attenuate those suspicions. But, young and adventurous, of course I didn't listen. While I didn't get much involved for a while, as a graduate student I began attending unprogrammed meetings. You know you're a nerd when your idea of living dangerously is hanging around with the wrong kind of Quakers! Be that as it may, I liked what I found there. What I found there was the same depth and sincerity of spiritual struggle, the same profound desire to know and do the will of God, the same sense of community and love that I had grown up with among Evangelical Friends, even if much of what was transpiring was inspired by different priorities, transacted under different names, spoken with a different dialect. There *were and are* important differences between the branches of Friends, serious differences,

---

41   The centrality of this notion to early Friends is highlighted in: Gerard Guiton, *The Early Quakers and the "Kingdom of God": Peace, Testimony and Revolution*, San Francisco: Inner Light Books, 2012.

and these should not, indeed cannot, be ignored or under-played. Friends between the branches, and *as often* within the branches too, genuinely disagree with one another, and on matters that matter. But despite those differences, there is no doubt in my mind and heart that both in the community of my youth, and in the community I have grown into as an adult, the Spirit is at work, and that I am among Friends. I have come to know and to love Liberal Friends as I have long known and loved more theologically Conservative Friends, and I am able to enter into meaningful worship in both contexts. I am a Christian Quaker, so I commune with joy among Evangelical and Orthodox Friends, but I have a progressive social agenda, so I am able to join enthusiastically with Liberal Friends in promoting that.[42] For me, though, I know I speak here out of my own experience, an experience I know is not shared by everybody, *both* are family.

Because of this I confess to being troubled, and quite hurt, when I hear Friends on each side of this "divide" maligning the other side, however subtly, even unknowingly. I am troubled, and quite hurt, when I hear Liberal Friends, sometimes even as part of a ministry in meeting, being dismissive of, even hostile to, Christianity, and more Orthodox Friends. And I am equally troubled, and hurt, when I hear Evangelical or Orthodox Friends, sometimes even from the pulpit, taking cheap swipes at "liberals" and "Liberal Friends." I know that people are vulnerable, and often in pain themselves, so mostly I try to suck it up, and not let it bother me too much. But often it does. Especially when it has a sharp edge. Especially when, in a flexing of our egos, we take these differences as an opportunity to

---

42   In fact, it is because I have a commitment to the gospel of Christ that I have a progressive social agenda—that's what I think follows from that commitment (although I know that not all Friends share that conclusion).

define ourselves *over against* the others, like the Pharisee in the gospel who prays: "God, thank you that I am not like one of those other people" (Luke 18:11, paraphrase). Especially when what is being said is not entirely true, or "true" in a way that is not really fair, that reduces a flesh and blood person to a few quick, unflattering indicators. In moments of frustration, I too still often succumb to such temptation myself (and in my case with Friends on both sides, so I am a worse offender than anyone!), and I am working on repenting of it.

One of the interesting and seductive things about caricatures is that they are based on real features, but these are exaggerated, and the rough outlines they present do not give us the subject's true character. That's why they are good for the purposes of humour, but inappropriate for genuine understanding. And that is also how caricatures are distinguished from portraits that are supposed to capture character, and are, therefore, not often funny. If a portrait makes you laugh, it is a bad portrait; if a caricature doesn't make you laugh, it is a bad caricature. Initiatives like Baltimore Yearly Meeting's inter-visitation program among Friends of different kinds is precisely an attempt to move us, with respect to each other, past the level of caricature, and on to portraiture, if not genuine Friendship. If nothing else, I find it something of a mockery of our peace testimony that while we want to encourage Jews and Palestinians, Tootsies and Hutus, Americans and Iranians, to work cooperatively across their differences, we Friends not only cannot often find a way to work together on worthwhile common projects, but can often not even find a way to *talk* meaningfully with each other. Though, of course, sometimes we do!

We tend, seemly by nature, to gravitate to those who already agree with us, which makes life a lot easier, and allows us to get on with things. As a philosopher, I am in-clined to move backwards, to question starting points rath-er than assume them. As the French, Jewish philosopher Emmanuel Levinas notes: the beginning of ethics is to be put into question. Only in the face of genuine difference are our self-certainties, and self-aggrandizements, and our thoughtless impositions of our own understandings upon others, shattered. We should be grateful for the one who challenges us. My conviction, right or wrong, is that we are richer in knowing one another, and in learning from one another—*especially* from those with whom we disagree. As Levinas puts it elsewhere: "only the other can teach me." Chances are that the person with whom I disagree is not deluded, but that they see something that I don't see; they, therefore, have something I need. That is, they have something to share with me that will deepen and broaden my own understanding and experience.

The unity of mutual commitment

We Quakers often struggle with the fact that, on so many issues of profound importance, we find ourselves out of unity with one another, and particularly with those of what we call the other branches. It is, therefore, worth thinking a bit about "unity." For we do indeed have a sense of unity that comes from the language of business meeting when we say we have come to unity when we all, or all of us who do not stand aside, consent that a particular deci-sion is in the will of God. In that sense unity does mean something like agreement (albeit, in traditional Quaker thinking this does not mean that we agree with each other, but that we agree with God, the true Quaker autocrat). But that is not the only, and perhaps not even the most import-ant, sense of the term. While not always easy to achieve, the unity of agreement is in some ways the cheapest form of unity. It is easy to be in unity with those with whom we agree. A deeper and more difficult form of unity is hanging in there with others precisely when we don't agree, and when the prospects of agreement are slim to none, when we are committed to one another *despite* disagreements, as anyone who has been in a long-term relationship knows. In this sense disagreement is not the end of unity, but its crucible, its most stringent test.

For most of us on most matters, including for most of Quaker history at least since the second third of the nineteenth century, the failure to reach unity of the first kind, the unity of agreement, has precipitated the loss of the second kind of unity, the unity of mutual commitment, as well. We have given up on unity, and gone our separate ways, each leaving the other to their own devices, and excesses. There is something good about that; each side is able to get on with things in a way that they couldn't before—and I don't want to downplay that genuine advantage. But I am suggesting that something is lost thereby as well: a broader sense of fraternity and sorority, but also a richness of opinion, and, perhaps most importantly, the necessity of patient imaginativeness in waiting worship with those with whom we disagree, seeking God's guidance for a way forth that cuts across the entrenched positions on both sides. We are, in my judgment, too quick as Quakers of diverse branches to take sides in what since at least the 1980s has been known as "the culture wars," Liberal Friends agreeing almost point for point with a left-wing political agenda, and accepting whatever implications they take that as having for religious life, and Evangelical and Orthodox Friends agreeing almost point for point with a right-wing theological agenda, and accepting whatever implications they take that as having for political life. At that point I'm not sure what function being a Quaker has to play in things, except as a backup for what we already want. Perhaps I am deluded (well, I am almost certainly deluded!), but somehow I expect more from us.

The spirit to which we attend should be neither the spirit of the left, nor the spirit of the right, but the Spirit of God. Seeking the guidance of that Spirit, the Spirit, especially with those with whom we disagree, is much harder than circling the wagons with those with whom we already agree, and requires a unity of mutual commitment prior to a unity of agreement—but that might be the only hope for a broader unity of agreement that undermines and transforms the current ideological divide that is tearing the larger social fabric, and the Quaker fabric with it, apart. What if rather than taking sides in the current ideological divide, and demonizing those on the other side, we were to sit worshipfully with those on the other side, and demonize the ideological divide? What a testimony *that* would be to the world! Part of my agenda this week is to plead for that testimony.

A living, dialectical tension

My more specific agenda, to this end, is to sketch out an understanding of Quakerism that will allow Quakers on both sides (on all sides!) to understand themselves, and those Quakers with whom they disagree, as exploiting legitimate and necessary trajectories within the space opened up by early Quakerism, and this so that we might see ourselves as belonging to, and relying upon, each other even across our very real and important disagreements. Rather than being settled in our concerns and reading these back into Quakerism as its essential core (and correlatively reading the concerns of other Friends out of the core as superfluous accidents or later impositions), I am attempting to read early Quakerism as the spiritual and conceptual space that opened up the possibility of the diverse interpretations Quakerism has undergone.

That is, what early Quakers held in a living, dialectical tension, has degenerated for contemporary Friends into two opposing camps. It was *because* early Quakers were uncompromisingly convinced of the Power of the Inward Christ to remake them that no static articulations of that Power, which they referred to as "outer," were considered adequate to it, which is why they were committed to the doctrine of continuing revelation. It was *because* early Quakers were "radical" in the sense of grounded in the essential, that they were "radical" in the sense of innovative and progressive. It was *because* early Quakers were rooted in Christianity that they were open to new Light. These two sides, held in dialectical tension by early Friends, a tension that was the very life, or spirit, of the fellowship, have become bifurcated for contemporary Friends, Orthodox Friends laying claim to the sense of radical that suggests rooted in foundations, and Liberal Friends embracing the sense of radical as pressing toward revolutionary change. While early Friends sought the fulfillment of Christianity, Orthodox Friends seek to preserve (rather than fulfill) it, and Liberal Friends tend toward leaving it behind.

Thus, "orthodox" (or evangelical) Friends, exploit and highlight the thoroughgoing commitment to Christ that animated early (and until quite recently, almost all of) Quakerism, but are perhaps too quick to identify in an unquestioning way the Christ of Quaker experience with the theologically constructed Christ of historical Christianity. Orthodox Friends, often quoting second generation Quakers anxious to ensure a persecuting culture that Quakers were indeed Christian, tend to overlook the fact that for early Friends the preceding 1600 years of Christian "ortho-doxy," "since [i.e., after] the apostles' days," were consid-ered to be lost in apostasy. The concern with creeds, the wedding of ecclesiastical and state power, the authority and enforcement of theological precepts—all of this was, in their phrase, "out of the Power." Orthodox Friends tend to overlook just how unorthodox early Quakers were. But this not because Friends desired to be unorthodox, not be-cause they took any perverse pride in being recalcitrant, but because they wanted to be *truly* orthodox, that is, they sought to ground their testimonies and teachings in the Truth, that is, in the Life and Power of God. But to do this they had to take definitive distance from the orthodoxy of the day, even as they called the so-called orthodox of the day to a deeper and genuine orthodoxy: obedience not to the Christ of human theological construct, but the Christ Within. Orthodoxy is, then, or at least I am suggesting, a genuine but partial expression of the Quaker way.

In an "equal but opposite" gesture, liberal Quakers, as the name suggests, revel in their liberation from tradition-al religious forms, which is entirely consistent with the founding inspiration of Quakerism. For many of us who have grown up in highly restrictive, even oppressive or abusive, religious communities, this freedom is like a fresh breath of mountain air after the suffocating closeness of authoritarianism. But what tends to be eclipsed in the ex-hilaration of this emancipatory emphasis is that the Quak-er freedom from authorities was, at least for early Friends, anything but the humanistic "freedom from" that leaves us obedient only to ourselves and our own best judg-ments, but a freedom necessary to a deeper and unequivo-cal obedience to the Inward Christ. Quaker freedom from worldly authorities was not freedom from authority; it was a freedom from worldly authorities for the sake of obedience to the true Authority. So Quaker business practices were never a question of seeking consensus, but of seeking God's will; "the sense of the meeting," the outcome of worshipful waiting upon the Spirit of God, was the *sign* of, and in no way a substitute for, God's leading. And this leading, moreover, was was never an expression of what I, or we, were comfortable with, or wanted. One of clearest signs for early Friends that a leading was from God was that, in their phrase, it was "a cross" to me, that it was precisely what I did not want, and that I was bound to obey it regardless, as the only way to be "released" (made free) from it. Liberality is another genuine, but partial, expression of the Quaker way.

Risky Christianity: losing and saving

My proposal in arguing for Quakerism as the fulfillment of Christianity (which early Quakers would have seen simply as true Christianity), in arguing for Quakerism as a radicalizing spirit, is to provide a framework in which Friends of each of our orientations can see themselves, but see themselves as functioning within a movement that is larger than any particular orientation by itself. I want to refer to these differing orientations as trajectories, suggesting that they are going somewhere, and from somewhere—more like energies within a larger field of force than static positions. If the more liberal side of Quakerism traces out a vector that leads out from the source into an ever new beyond (a centrifugal force straining toward new light, a universalizing force that sketches out the way of innovation), the more orthodox side of Quakerism traces out a vector that seeks to renew itself ever again from the roots (a centripetal force that brings us back to draw living water from reliable sources). For early Friends, these were not two divergent paths, but integrated and complementary trajectories, aspects of the same living Spirit, integrated moments within the life of the Spirit.

And if we want to renew the famous Quaker tree metaphor, though here perhaps turning it on its side, we might say that Liberal Friends revel in the "fruits" of the Quaker tradition, while orthodox Friends attend to the "roots." That, of course, is a vast generalization, as liberals too are interested in roots, and the orthodox have picked some fine fruits. But as an image it perhaps works at a certain level. But as I well know having grown up on Cherry Street, a fruitful tree requires both of these aspects: perpetual renewal and new growth, where these two aspects are part of one and the same process. If we don't attend to the roots, the seasons for Quaker fruits will be few (which is what I think, metaphorically speaking, may be happening to many of our liberal meetings), and if we are too exclusively oriented to the roots, we become fearful of allowing new fruits to come to maturity, pruning vital, fresh branches with reckless caution (which is what I think is happening in many of our orthodox meetings).

My proposal that we think of Quakerism as a fulfillment of Christianity might then be restated as follows: "Just as Jesus's relationship to the law is an expression of the law that puts the law at risk, so Quakerism is *an expression of Christianity*, but one in which *Christianity itself is put at risk*." In light of this formula, liberal Quakers will no doubt accuse me of trying to keep Christ at the centre of Quakerism, even as Orthodox Friends will no doubt accuse me of selling out Christ. Indeed, I am trying to maintain the uncomfortable position where both accusations might be true.

Thinking Quakerism as an expression of "Christianity in which Christianity is at risk" is a tricky proposition, because it opens up the very real possibility that Quakerism might exceed Christianity itself. One is then faced with the peculiar prospect that the most faithful expression of Christianity is no longer necessarily Christian, at least not in any recognizable sense. Just as fulfilling the law puts the law at risk, but for the sake of the law, so a genuinely fulfilled Christianity puts Christianity itself at risk, but for the sake of the way of Christ. For those of us with an attachment to Christianity, that is a frightful prospect, even as it liberates us for "fresh winds of the Spirit," and opens us to new Light. But that is, I am suggesting, not only a Quaker reading of Christianity (albeit one that I think Quakers have undertaken particularly well), but is at the very heart of Christianity itself. As Christ himself puts it: "For whosoever will save his life shall lose it; and whosoever will lose his life for my sake shall find it" (Matthew 16:25, KJV).[43] What of the law must we lose in order to save it, and what of Christianity must we lose to find it, to find it again, not according to the letter, but in Spirit and in Truth?

The diversity of Friends

To be clear, I am not advocating here for the administrative unification of Friends; our diversity is a strength, and we should neither fear it, nor bemoan it. It is essential, I think, that the diverse branches of Friends remain true to their character, and faithful to their respective callings. We can each play our roles within a larger drama without reducing the larger drama to our particular role within it. There are aspects of genuine Quaker work that liberals will always be better at doing than Orthodox

---

43   The larger passage has to do with giving up one's identity to follow Jesus. Might that mean a willingness to give up one's Christian identity too? To the extent that that identity is an impediment to living out the gospel, I venture it does.

Friends, and aspects of genuine Quaker work that the Orthodox will excel at better than the liberals.[44] What I *do* advocate, what I *am* suggesting, is that maybe we can each see ourselves, *and* those of the other branches, as living out a legitimate and faithful trajectory within Quakerism within the purview of a broader viewpoint, thus not as two solitudes, or even as divergent branches, but as each tracing out a course within a shared field of force. Such would allow for mutual recognition, even mutual appreciation, without insisting upon agreement, and without compromising our particular convictions and emphases. Such would allow Orthodox Friends to appreciate and celebrate the freedom upon which the gospel opens and that Liberal Friends enjoy, as it would allow Liberal Friends to appreciate and respect the devoted embrace of that "freedom giving gospel" practiced by the Orthodox—even if we continue to disagree about who has already gone too far, and who has not yet gone far enough. Such would allow for an attenuation of the sometimes bitter, parochial, and polarizing debates over who are the real inheritors of Quakerism, and who are the impostors. The point would not be to put an end to conversations over the essence of Quakerism, but to open them up. I am not suggesting we paper over our disagreements, that we do not have the debates we must have, but that we do so in a different spirit—in a radicalizing spirit that understands that innovation is *both* the fruit of groundedness *and* a perpetual challenge to it. And such would deepen the appreciation for, and willingness to engage in—rather than what is currently almost universal suspicion from both sides—those painfully difficult but noble initiatives to bring Friends of diverse ori-

---

44   I would also want to speak for a unique place of ministry and testimony for Conservative [Wilberite] Friends, although I have unjustifiably not given them their due in these lectures.

entations together for shared work and worship: Friends World Committee for Consultation, Friends United Meeting, Canadian Friends Service Committee, American Friends Service Committee, Friends Council for National Legislation, Earlham School of Religion, United Society of Friends Women International, Pendle Hill, and others. Such would help us, perhaps, to overcome our dogmatism on both sides (and there *is* dogmatism on both sides), on all sides, and be teachable, that is, to be open to the leadership of the Spirit, or to be Friends. That is, perhaps, only a crazy dream. But maybe crazy ones are the only dreams really worth dreaming.

Discussion Questions/Queries:
Quakerism: A House Divided

Are we, in our own meetings, actively open to hearing the experience and "teachings" of Friends from other branches, actively concerned to exclude them, indifferent to them, or simply ignorant of them? What steps might we take to facilitate such opportunities for learning that, while it might "challenge" us, would not "threaten" our own integrity of conviction? What are the potential advantages, and possible disadvantages, of inter-branch Quaker dialogue and cooperation?

Do we define who we are as a community "positively" (that is, in terms of who we are), or "negatively" (that is, as over against others from whom we hope to distinguish ourselves)? Is the one possible without the other? What are the implications of an emphasis on one of these, or the other, both in terms of how we think about ourselves, and in terms of how we relate to others?

Are our understandings of others founded in caricature, or portraiture? What would allow us to move from one to the other? If we base our understanding of others in caricature, do we risk becoming merely a caricature ourselves? What would be the advantages of moving forward toward more nuanced views of ourselves and others as complex and complicated human beings—all struggling to make the best of things from the site in which we find ourselves? What would need to happen to facilitate that?

What does it mean to be "in unity"? Does unity require agreement? How might we seek unity even when we are not in agreement? What are the potential advantages of conceiving of unity outside of agreement? Is agreement still the ultimate goal, the "true" unity, or is disagreement an integral aspect of any genuine unity?

In what ways is the tension between the different branches of Friends (or even some of tensions internal to branches!) a mere reflection of larger societal and cultural tensions? Is there anything specific to Quakers in how we hold these tensions, and how we attempt to work them out? What steps might we take to allow our differences to enrich us as the larger Society of Friends, rather than to divide, and to diminish us?

Is it helpful to see the development of the different branches of Friends as (among other factors) the accenting of certain aspects of the tradition and the eclipsing of others? Which aspects of early Quakerism do you and your group latch on to and privilege, and which aspects do you tend to gloss over as no longer important, or as no longer relevant? What is gained by the focus on certain aspects at the expense of others, and what is lost in doing this? What might we learn about who *we* are by exposing ourselves to the emphases of branches not our own?

Can looking to early Friends help us to understand the different trajectories traced out by later developments as potentially complementary to one another rather than necessarily in opposition to each other? Is it possible to translate the early Quaker "dialectic" between "rootedness" and "radicalness" in ways that would be meaningful for us today?

The idea that in order to be faithful to its own calling, Christianity might have to press even beyond itself, is certainly a controversial suggestion, and one that is potentially highly threatening to Christian Quakers (including to the author of these lectures!). But do Christians serve Christianity, or serve Christ? And if it is the case that Jesus felt the need to exceed the religious conventions of his day in order to fulfill them, are there instances where we are called to do the same today (regardless of which branch we come from)? Insofar as (some) Liberal Friends perceive themselves as already having gone beyond the particularities of Christian expression, does their doing so tie them back into the dynamic instituted by Jesus (and replicated by early Quakers), perhaps in a way they may have lost sight of? Is being caught up in this push-pull "dialectic" something that Friends from across the theological spectrum share, even if we variously emphasize different aspects of it?

What would it look like for Liberal Friends, and Orthodox/ Evangelical Friends, and Conservative Friends, to be in a healthy, blessed, and peaceful relationship with each other? Is that possible? Is that desirable? What steps can we take to get closer to that?

(Love) is the sweetness of life. It is the sweet, tender, melting nature of God, flowing up through his seed of life into the creature, and of all things making the creature most like unto himself, both in nature and operation. It fulfils the Law, it fulfils the Gospel; it wraps up all in one, and bring forth all in the oneness. It excludes all evil out of the heart, it perfects all good in the heart. A touch of Love does this in measure, perfect love does this in fullness.

— Isaac Penington, *Some of the Mysteries of God's Kingdom Glanced At*, 1663.

Lecture Five:
The Love of Knowledge

Radicalizing knowledge

I began the week with the Bible, on Monday, reading Jesus's relationship to the law as one neither of obedience nor disobedience, but of fulfillment. I followed the next day, with a reading of early Quakerism as taking up a relationship to the Christianity of its day as reiterating this relationship, that is, as one that was neither a straightforward adherence nor a rejection of Christianity, but an attempt at its fulfillment. In the third lecture I attempted (having recourse to turf closer to my own) to provide what might be called a loose, philosophical analysis of this structure of fulfillment, relabelling it "radicalizing spirit," suggesting that human life, both at an individual and a group level, traces out a structure that parallels it. Yesterday I explored how we might understand the thorny issue of the contemporary relationship between Quakerism and Christianity by reading it through this lens, in an attempt to provide a theoretical scaffolding upon which to understand the Quaker movement as, to borrow the phrase of Ashworth and Wildwood, "Rooted in Christianity; Open to new light." I want today to conclude by returning to the Bible,[45] to trace out once more this structure of fulfillment, or radicalizing spirit, this time with respect to the crucial issue of knowledge. I do so because what we think we know

---

45   I would suggest that I have never really left the realm of the Biblical, but return to it today in a more straightforward and explicit way.

is so often at the bottom of what divides us. Orthodox Friends claim to "know" what has been revealed to them in the Scriptures, and contextualize whatever other knowledge claims are made across experience or science in light of that, whereas modern Liberal Friends lean toward trusting their own experience as the basis of what they claim to know religiously (although this is usually taken as being quite tentative[46]), and rely upon the powers of human reason (i.e., science) for the knowledge of everything else. Religious claims that don't pass the muster of these tests are suspect, which is most of them. If what we "know" divides us, perhaps we need to rethink knowledge in light of a radicalizing spirit. Perhaps knowledge itself needs to be fulfilled. I want to suggest that this is precisely what Paul attempts to do in his first letter to the Corinthians.

Behold, all things are become new

Indeed, I would propose that the structure of fulfillment, that I am also referring to with the more Quakerly resonate locution "radicalizing spirit," is not an occasional thing in the Christian Scriptures, popping up here and there, but is all-pervasive, is the very dynamic of the gospel itself. If that is true, the gospel is not used but abused when it is taken to prop up one side of an ideological struggle, and to demonize the other side. Orthodox and Liberal Friends are both guilty of this, as am I. Rather, what the structure of fulfillment offers is the promise of life for all, beyond the morally lazy practice of dividing the world up between the white hats and the black hats, toward what some have described, and not so badly I think, as a "radi-

---

46   Dandelion astutely refers to this stance as the "absolute perhaps." Pink Dandelion, *An Introduction to Quakerism*, Cambridge: Cambridge University Press, 2007, pp. 151-3.

cal third way." Neither this, nor that, but something else, something that gets us unstuck, not polarized, but energized. To encounter the Gospel then, to read it as a promise, is to be open to being surprised. The Good *News*, as the name suggests, is something *new*, specifically not the same old thing, specifically not what is expected. In order, then, to hear the Gospel, to really hear it, with ears to hear, is to be attuned to the promise of fulfillment.

We have already seen this at work, in the opening lecture. When confronted by the man with the withered hand, planted by the Pharisees to trip him up, Jesus does not follow the straight line of the law and refuse to work on the Sabbath, but rather heals the man. But this Jesus does not refer to as breaking the law, as do the Pharisees who see only two options at this point, either to keep the law or to violate it. Jesus claims, instead, neither to have kept nor broken the law, but to have fulfilled it. The Pharisees didn't see that coming!

But we find this same dynamic in many other Biblical stories as well:

When presented with the woman caught in adultery (John 8: 1-11), another trap, to see if he would condemn her, as any straight-laced and straight thinking Jewish rabbi would be compelled to do, Jesus slips the question of condemnation altogether, ignores the line that runs from sin to condemnation, and then, and *only after that*, to forgiveness. Rather, Jesus begins at the end, with forgiveness, which changes not only the expected chronology of events, but transforms the events themselves. For here, where forgiveness is pronounced independently of confession, prior to confession, confession becomes possible because it is no longer the sinner's participation in his or her own condemnation, but the possibility of taking a fuller responsibility for the life now restored. The Pharisees didn't see that one coming either. That's fulfillment.

When the disciples informed Jesus of the hunger of the crowds by the Sea of Galilee (Matthew 14: 13-21), the disciples sage counsel was that the multitudes should be sent away to seek sustenance. But Jesus took and blessed and broke the contents of a boy's boxed lunch and transformed them into a feast for five-thousand, with more to spare. The miraculous is the unexpected, the un-anticipatable, and the unexpected itself is a miracle, a break with the necessary, which, far from being mere magic, is rather the deeper structure from which even the dream of magic takes its bearings. The line stretched between the options of staying and being hungry and going for food is transformed into neither, but into the filling, the fulfillment, of all. Even the disciples didn't see that coming.

For in the Gospel, it is not merely that roads do not lead to anticipated destinations, they may not lead to destinations at all; premises not only do not necessarily lead to logical conclusions, they sometimes lead to something entirely other than conclusions; and it is not only that even straight arrows do not hit their intended targets, arrows and the targets are frequently configured into something else. Water becomes wine (John 2: 1-11); one is not baptized with water, but with fire and the Holy Spirit (Matthew 3:11); and swords are beaten into plowshares (Isaiah 2:4)—which, before it is a task for the blacksmith, is a supreme exercise in imagination, in the miraculous. The supposedly straight lines that should lead from expectation to realization, the seeming logicality that draws us—perhaps inexorably—from anticipation to consummation, when exposed to the Gospel, are often, not always (for that would make the unexpected expected again), but often, transformed into something else.

How do we envision this? It is not exactly that the line that leads from A to B is eliminated; the law is not erased by Jesus. It is not that the expectations are disappointed exactly; it is more that they are reconfigured. It is rather that what is—the law, forgiveness, loaves and fishes—are re-visioned in the light of a new perspective, are re-contextualized to the point of becoming something other than what they previously were, becoming something entirely new. "Behold, all things are become new," Paul writes (2 Corinthians 5:17). The Gospel is revolutionary to the point of transforming, re-new-ing, reality itself; which is perhaps why in Acts there is talk of turning the world upside down (Acts 17:6), and perhaps why Christians can speak of being in but not of the world, not capitulating to the inevitabilities imposed by what is "real-istic." The Gospel calls for expectation, hope, and the realization of what is not the case. And perhaps "the world" that the Christian Bible opposes to the Gospel is our inability or unwillingness to see and live expansively, to imagine a bigger picture; perhaps "the world" is a narrowing, a reduction, the monotony of the same that always follows the same, the "all is vanity" of Ecclesiastes (1:2, 12:8), over against the Gospel that re-forms, that incites and excites. Perhaps "the world" that is opposed to the gospel is no particular set of structures or practices, but capitulation in the face of the ineluctable necessity of law, or, otherwise put, a lack of imagination, being closed to the Spirit of God. It is in this sense, perhaps, that the Gospel opposes itself to the law. Not constrained by the expectations provided by the Sabbath legalities, nor by the psycho-juridical order of confession and forgiveness, nor by the physical laws of loaves and fishes—the Gospel is the promise of renewal because it is "true to life," and life itself is unpredictable, and requires for living it well (that is, faithfully) imaginative work. If this were psychology, we'd be talking about a new gestalt, if theology, transcendence, if science, we'd be talking about a paradigm shift, if politics, revolution. And we are talking about all of these, and more.

Whether there be knowledge, it shall vanish away

What I want to suggest is that when it comes to the Gospel's treatment of knowledge we should not be surprised if we are surprised, should not be surprised if our conventional expectations regarding knowledge are not also undermined and transformed in the light of the Gospel. This is, I propose, precisely what we find in 1 Corinthians 13, Paul's gorgeous hymn to love, which has a surprisingly lot to say about knowledge. I pick this passage because of its familiarity, because even if you are not a regular reader of the Bible, you've been to weddings, where it is regularly read, and appropriately so, for, unlike Celine Dion's "Titanic theme song" or Whitney Houston's "I Will Always Love You," staples at weddings during their season, this chapter never becomes hackneyed.

Although for the sake of my lecture today I will focus on the later verses, 8 to 13, which focus on the function and fate of knowledge, and I will read the whole chapter, in the familiar locutions of the King James Version:

> Though I speak with the tongues of men and of angels, and have not love, I am become as sounding brass, or a tinkling cymbal. 2. And though I have the gift of prophecy, and understand all mysteries, and all knowledge; and though I have all faith, so that I could remove mountains, and have not love, I am nothing. 3. And though I bestow all my goods to feed the poor, and though I give my body to be burned, and have not

love, it profiteth me nothing. 4. Love suffereth long and is kind; love envieth not; love vaunteth not itself, is not puffed up, 5. Doth not behave itself unseemly, seeketh not her own, is not easily provoked, thinketh no evil; 6. Rejoiceth not in iniquity, but rejoiceth in the truth; 7. Beareth all things, believeth all things, hopeth all things, endureth all things.

Now, I ask you to listen for the references to knowledge in what remains:

Love never faileth: but whether there be prophecies, they shall fail; whether there be tongues, they shall cease; *whether there be knowledge, it shall vanish away.* 9. For *we know in part*, and we prophesy in part. 10. But when that which is perfect is come, then that which is in part shall be done away. 11. When I was a child, I spake as a child, *I understood as a child, I thought as a child*: but when I became a man, I put away childish things. 12. For *now we see through a glass, darkly; but then face to face*: now I *know in part*: but then shall I *know even as I am known.* 13. And now abideth faith, hope, and love (*agape* in the Greek[47]); but the greatest of these is love.

Now, we are dealing here (in verse 9) with a knowledge that is partial, which is opposed (in verse 10) to that which is perfect. We are dealing (in verse 11) with an immature knowledge, which is opposed by a subsequent maturity. We are dealing (in verse 12) with a "seeing" (which is at least a *kind* of knowledge) that is "through a glass" (the Greek word is "*einigmati*," from which we get our word "enigma"), seeing in darkness, that is, a seeing poorly,

---

47   While the King James Bible translates *agape* here as "charity," I have opted for "love."

which is opposed to seeing "face to face." We are dealing yet again (in verse 12) with a partial knowledge, which is this time opposed to a knowing "as I am known."

We are dealing, in short, with a movement, cast eschatologically, that is, from what is the case to what is to be accomplished. On the side of "what is the case," we find: partial knowledge; childish understanding and thinking; seeing enigmatically, that is, in obscurity, and in darkness; and, again, partial knowledge.

Now, on our normal way of thinking, according to our expectations, we should expect these examples of insufficient knowledge to be completed by a fully sufficient, or complete, knowledge. We would expect partial knowledge to find its completion in full knowledge. We would expect childish knowledge to find its completion in adult knowledge. We would expect seeing through a glass darkly to find its completion in seeing clearly, and seeing in darkness to find its fulfillment by a seeing in perfect light. We would expect the repeat of partial knowledge to again find its fulfillment in total knowledge.

But listen to what we *do* get; and notice that (with one exception, which we will have to discuss) the word "knowledge" does not appear in the list: in the place of partial knowledge we do not get full knowledge, as we would normally expect, but "the coming of the perfect:" in the place of childish understanding and thinking we do not get adult understanding and thinking, as we would normally expect, but becoming a man; in the place of seeing enigmatically, and seeing in darkness, we do not get seeing clearly, and in the light, as we would normally expect, but seeing "face to face;" in the place of partial knowledge mentioned here for the second time, our normal expectation of full knowledge again is not what is promised, but rather, knowing "as I am known."

That is, the expected trajectory, running from partial to full knowledge, from knowing in part to knowing perfectly, is, in this text, subverted. Incomplete knowledge is not completed, fulfilled, perfected, in more or more perfect knowledge, but in something else altogether, something that is not knowledge at all, and doesn't have to do with knowledge, at least not directly. The perfection of knowledge is not a supreme knowledge; rather, the whole task of knowing is subverted, and displaced, by something that is not in its turn a matter of knowledge at all. Allow me to put this as startlingly as possible: the perfection of knowledge is precisely in its being overturned! As a philosopher, I didn't see that coming! But as readers of the Gospel, as ones prepared to be on guard for the structure of fulfillment, we should not be entirely shocked, since already in verse 8, right before this new and unexpected trajectory is given, we were already told that knowledge would pass away.

And if there was any question as to what it is that knowledge, under the auspices of the Gospel, would evolve into as it comes to perfection, we are surely given the response in both the verse that precedes this re-visioning of the trajectory of knowledge, and in the one that follows: in both verses 8 and 13 the passing away of knowledge has as its context the non-passing away, the non-failure, of love.

And if this is the case, then two phrases in our passage can be more fully understood: what it means to see "face to face," and what it means to "know even as I also am known."

For recall that in lieu of our present, enigmatic knowledge, the promise, the goal, is seeing "face to face," which I am suggesting is not just another way of saying "seeing clearly," but a revolutionary re-visioning. Now, we are all familiar with the difference between knowing about someone, having knowledge about them, and actually meeting them. I could take several hours to tell you everything I know about my mother, and then have her brother come in and do the same, to tell you things about my mother that would surprise even me, but even after several hours of instruction, if I were to ask you: "Do you know my mother?" most of you would have to say: "Well, I know a lot *about* your mother, but I don't *know* her. I've never met her." A face to face relationship is not one qualified by the knowledge of facts. It is the not the relationship between a knowing subject and a known object. A face to face relationship is personal. It is a relationship between subjects, a two-way relationship, and one wherein the "knowledge" of each other is not about facts, but about intimacy. Face to face is the posture of intimacy, the posture of lovers, of interlocutors, and also the posture of combatants: which is why we can love God, speak with God, wrestle with God, as we can love our intimate, speak with our intimate, and wrestle with our intimate, things that are impossible to do with mere things that we *know about*, because all of these require someone who will love, and speak, and wrestle back. And it is this relationship that the Bible refers to as "knowing" when it is using that term in its most important sense. When Adam "knew" his wife Eve and they conceived a child, they were not engaged in an intellectual exercise! This was a face to face relationship; this was intimate familiarity.

That is why the passage continues: "At present I know in part, but then I shall know fully, even as I am also known." The final goal, here eschatologically cast, is "to know as I am known." And so "knowledge" is not entirely destroyed, even if the only knowledge that survives the passing away of knowledge is the kind that correlates to God's knowledge of me: and this knowledge in turn is best understood as the knowledge of the face to face, as a knowledge that *is* love—and why this discourse on knowledge is not out of place in Paul's great hymn to love. Yes, God knows the number of the hairs on my head, as the gospel of Matthew attests (10:30), but not in the manner of some supercomputer, coldly and impassively tabulating and calculating, knowing for the sake of knowing. Rather, God knows the number of hairs on my head to glory in my development through infancy, to embrace me in my insecurities at balding and aging, and to love me through the chemotherapy that reduces the count to null. The facts, by themselves, are enigmatic, pointless, meaningless, passing away, open to any sense we might choose to project upon them. They only become "knowledge," in the only sense that the Bible cares about on my view, when they are personal. The fullness of knowledge, its perfection, or fulfillment, is not more facts, but intimacy, the personal, and an intimacy that transforms the very meaning of the facts themselves.

Here, then, in a remarkable turn, the fulfillment of knowledge is not omniscience, but love, and in light of this our usual obsessions with "getting it right" are but a shadowy and ethereal distraction. And this is why, in the New Testament, not many wise are called (1 Corinthians 1:26); they are looking in the wrong place. And this is why Christian education, and Quaker education insofar as it effects its aspiration to fulfill Christianity, cannot be the mere learning of more, or even different, facts—but a knowing differently, in a different mode, by an entirely different measure. It is not that "knowledge as knowing about" is irrelevant, at least not at present, but we only participate in the Spirit of God when the end, that is the purpose, of our knowledge, is love. And this is why neither theology, nor science, and above all not philosophy, can be the key to knowledge—all of these are a part of the "in part," are what will pass away, in deference to the knowledge that is, in the end, love itself. And if we don't *know* that, if we don't *know* in that way, then, it seems to me, we have become, as the first verse of this chapter informs us, but as sounding brass or a tinkling cymbal.

Bear the burden of each other's failings, and pray for one another

I have been engaged his week in encouraging us as Quakers to know one another, and I have done a fair bit of theoretical work (probably too much!) to provide a framework in which we might understand ourselves and other Friends with whom we disagree on important matters as nevertheless fellow participants in the same radicalizing spirit that is the Quaker faith. What I hope to have suggested today is that this understanding, this knowledge, is only fulfilled as love. That, of course, is the hard part, but, in the end, the only part that really matters, the only part that endures.

Let me close the week with one of the British Yearly Meeting *Advices and Queries* that I suggest we think not only in the context of our own meetings, but as a way of approaching the larger body of Friends. It says what I have been trying to say much better than I have been saying it (and in a single paragraph!), and is, I think, a wonderful example of Quakerism as defined by William Penn, "Christianity writ plain."

"How can we make the meeting a community in which each person is accepted and nurtured, and strangers are welcome? Seek to know one another in the things which are eternal, bear the burden of each other's failings and pray for one another. As we enter with tender sympathy into the joys and sorrows of each other's lives, ready to give help and to receive it, our meeting can be a channel for God's love and forgiveness."[48]

To that I can only add: amen!

---

48   *Advices & Queries*, London: The Yearly Meeting of the Religious Society of Friends (Quakers) in Britain, 1995, #18, p. 10.

Discussion Questions/Queries:
The Love of Knowledge

What does the Bible mean by "knowledge"? How important is what we "know" to the faith that we live? If we were to think of knowledge differently, how might that affect the way we live out our faith?

Is it possible to read the Bible not as a "backup" for our own preferred points of view, but as a call beyond any and every ideological entrenchment toward something else? Why are some of us so tempted to "prove" our points by reference to the Bible? Is it possible to "know" the "truth" about things directly from the Bible? That is, is the Bible to be thought of principally as a book of "facts" about things? Or does the Bible itself point us toward a different kind of "knowledge," and a different kind of "truth"? And if so, might this re-open the Bible to some who reject it based on the perceived incredulity of its "facts"?

What other Biblical stories or themes could we read as presenting us not with the expected, with a pre-given either-or, but, through fulfillment, lead us beyond to a "radical third way"? Is the gospel message (the "good news") that we need not be "stuck" in our either-or dead-ends, but, through grace, find an opening beyond them? In what ways are we (as the broader Society of Friends, as a culture) "stuck" in either-or dilemmas, and what might getting beyond these look like?

The author here reads the Biblical opposition between "the world" and "the gospel" as the difference between being stuck in structures that divide and paralyze us, on the one hand, and the invitation to imaginatively and expansively break through to a shared participation in the love of God. Is this a credible aspect (among others) of this distinction? What should our relationship, as Quakers, be to the structures that "the world" imposes upon us? How are we to effectively be "in but not of" the world?

The author argues that, according to I Corinthians 13, the "per-fection" (i.e., the "fulfillment") of knowledge does not result in full or in perfect knowledge, but in love, namely, in a "face to face" relationship wherein we "know even as we are known." If this is the case, should "love" be the measure, the standard, for everything we claim to know? How might we test our knowledge according to the standards of love? What would this look like in our communities? What might the implications of this be for education? What might the implications of this be for how we relate to those (and particularly to fellow Friends) with whom we disagree?

What does the query with which the lectures close mean to you—personally, and as a local meeting—regarding how we as Friends, across the diverse theological and social spectrums we inhabit, might most effectively minister to one another?

CPSIA information can be obtained
at www.ICGtesting.com
Printed in the USA
LVOW10s2001050117

519875LV00002B/322/P